INTERWAY

Englisch für berufliche Schulen

Workbook

von
Rosemary King
Wolfgang Rosenkranz
Graham Tucker

Ernst Klett Verlag
Stuttgart Düsseldorf Leipzig

INTERWAY
Englisch für berufliche Schulen
Workbook

von

Rosemary King M.A., Fachlehrerin für Englisch an der Berufsbildenden Schule, Wesel;

Wolfgang Rosenkranz, Diplom-Handelslehrer, Oberstudienrat an der Freiherr-vom-Stein-Schule, Bad Oeynhausen;

Graham Tucker, B.A., Fachleiter für Englisch an der Berufsbildenden Schule, Castrop-Rauxel

Umschlaggestaltung
Friedemann Bröckel

Werkübersicht	
Student's Book	Klett-Nr. 809360
Workbook	Klett-Nr. 809370
Teacher's Book	Klett-Nr. 809380
Cassette	Klett-Nr. 809390

Gedruckt auf Recyclingpapier, hergestellt aus 100 % Altpapier.

1. Auflage 1 ³ 2 1 | 2000 1999 98

Alle Drucke dieser Auflage können im Unterricht nebeneinander benutzt werden, sie sind untereinander unverändert. Die letzte Zahl bezeichnet das Jahr dieses Druckes.
Dieses Werk folgt der reformierten Rechtschreibung und Zeichensetzung.

© Ernst Klett Verlag GmbH, Stuttgart 1998.
Alle Rechte vorbehalten.

Redaktion: Inge Spaughton

Druck: Gutmann + Co., Talheim
Printed in Germany.

ISBN 3-12-809370-9

Contents · Inhalt

Introduction · Vorwort		4
Unit 1	Living	5
Unit 2	Making choices	9
Unit 3	Working lives	14
Unit 4	Healthy eating	19
Unit 5	Healthy living	24
Unit 6	Fact or fiction?	29
Unit 7	Looking ahead	32
Unit 8	Making plans	37
Unit 9	Making arrangements	42
Unit 10	Superstitions and customs	46
Unit 11	Prejudices	50
Unit 12	What's on?	54
Unit 13	In black and white	58
Unit 14	Rules and regulations	62
Unit 15	Success and failure	66
Unit 16	Does age matter?	69
Unit 17	Going green!	74
Unit 18	Play the game!	79
Unit 19	Dangerous developments	83
Unit 20	Passport to the world	87

Commercial correspondence
Handelskorrespondenz

Enquiry	92
Offer	94
Order	96
Acknowledgement of order	98
Reminder	100
Complaint	102

Acknowledgements · Quellennachweis   104

Introduction · Vorwort

Mit diesem *Workbook* zum Lehrwerk INTERWAY können Sie das im Unterricht Gelernte wiederholen, vertiefen und festigen.

Die **Units 1 – 20** im ersten Teil dieses Buches entsprechen der Reihenfolge der Units im *Student's Book*.

Jede Unit im *Workbook* beinhaltet u. a.
- abwechslungsreiche Wortschatzübungen
- motivierende Grammatikübungen
- auf das Thema der Unit bezogene deutsch-englische Übersetzungen.

Die **Commercial correspondence** im zweiten Teil dieses Buches umfasst Übungen zur Korrespondenz der wichtigsten Geschäftsvorgänge mit ungestörten und gestörten Geschäftsabläufen *(Enquiry, Offer, Order, Acknowledgement of order, Reminder, Complaint)*. Dieser Teil ist insbesondere für kaufmännische Berufsfachschulen gedacht.

Die Einführung in die einzelnen Geschäftsabläufe erfolgt jeweils anhand der *Useful phrases*, die nach dem Baustein-Prinzip zusammengestellt wurden. Sie dienen der Erweiterung der Ausdrucksmöglichkeiten sowie der schnellen Orientierung bei der Musterkorrespondenz. Im Anschluss an die oben aufgeführten Geschäftsvorgänge folgen Übungen unterschiedlicher Art, die der Vertiefung und Festigung dienen.

Viel Spaß und Erfolg bei der Arbeit mit diesem Buch wünschen Ihnen

Autorin, Autoren und Redaktion

Unit 1 Living

Exercise 1 · The new flat

A friend of yours is interested in a flat.
Look at the following plan of the flat and then give the correct information.
Start with *There is / isn't ...* or *It has / hasn't got ...*

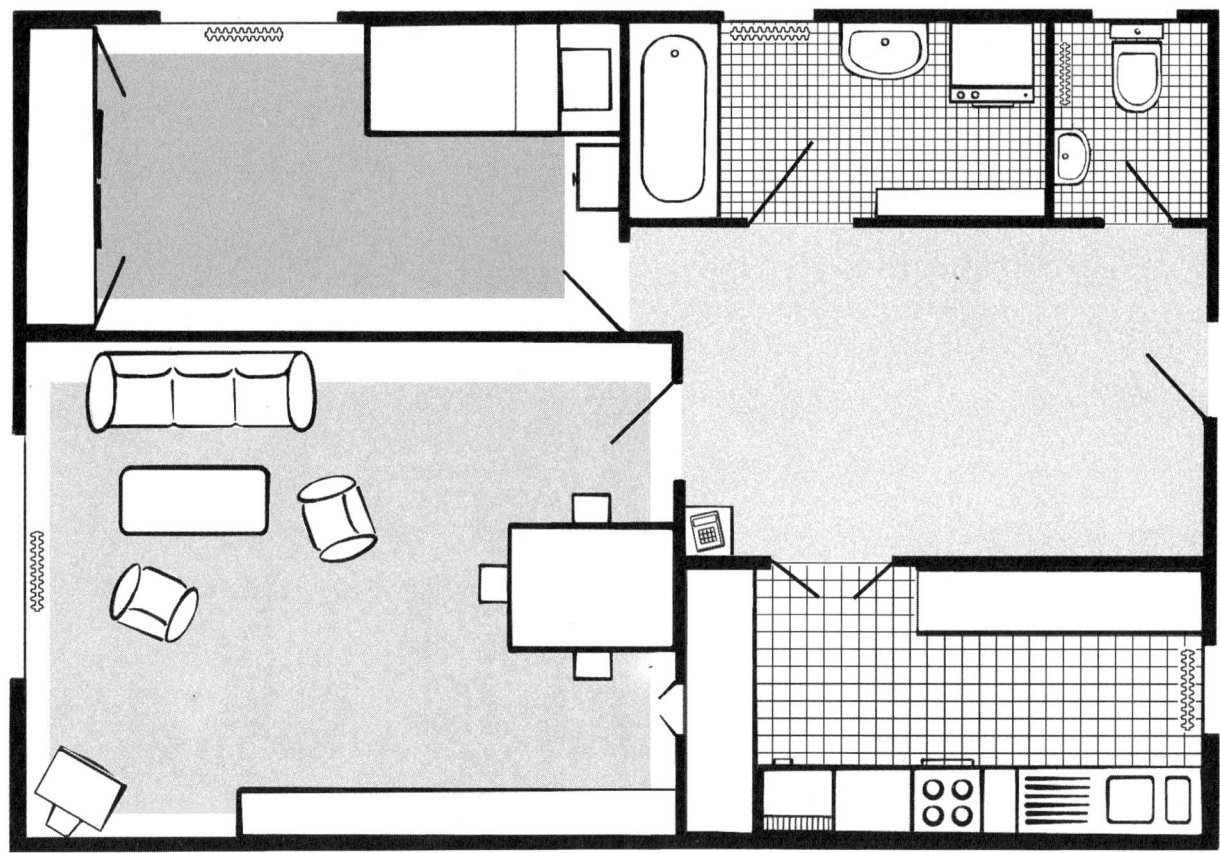

1. telephone? __There is a telephone in the hall._____
2. double bed? __It hasn't got a double bed in the bedroom._____
3. fridge? There _____.
4. central heating? It _____.
5. dining table? It _____.
6. cable / satellite TV? There _____.
7. wardrobe? It _____.
8. microwave oven? There _____.
9. toilet in the bathroom? It _____.
10. washing machine? There _____.

Exercise 2 · Situations, facts and habits

Look at the following pictures. Then match all the parts of the sentences.
Use the verbs in the box in the Present Simple.

1

2

3

4

5

6

share	her bike after work
not smoke	their flat
live	English at college
not tidy up	from England
learn	a flat with her friend
ride	in this house
not come	classical music
travel	to work by bus
not listen to	cigarettes
do the ironing	in the lounge

7

8

9

10

1. *Sandra rides her bike after work.*
2. The Browns _____.
3. Some people _____.
4. We _____.
5. Max and Ann _____.
6. Harry _____.
7. We _____.
8. James _____.
9. May Dlamini _____.
10. Lynn _____.

6 ■ *six*

Exercise 3 · Why? What? Where?

Ask questions about the underlined words.
Use the Present Simple and the question words below.

1. Maggie shares <u>a flat</u> with some friends.
2. She lives <u>in London</u>.
3. They <u>never</u> tidy up the flat.
4. They pay <u>£50 a week</u> for their flat.
5. Nicola gets on <u>well</u> with her flatmates.
6. Laura often does <u>the ironing</u>.
7. Jim always leaves the dirty dishes <u>in the sink</u>.
8. He likes <u>Heavy Metal</u> music.
9. Sarah and Alice travel to college <u>by bus</u>.
10. They don't go out often <u>because they haven't got much money</u>.

How?
Why?
What?
Where?
What kind of?
How often?
How much?

1. *What does Maggie share with some friends?*
2. _____?
3. _____?
4. _____?
5. _____?
6. _____?
7. _____?
8. _____?
9. _____?
10. _____?

Exercise 4 · What goes where?

4 a) Put the words from the box under the correct heading.

1. **Accommodation**

   cottage
   _____
   _____

cottage   station   flat
tidy up   rent   basement
post office   shop   bus
do the washing-up   train
roof   do the ironing
cellar   tram

4. **Public transport**

   _____
   _____
   _____

2. **Housework**

   _____
   _____
   _____

3. **Parts of the house**

   _____
   _____
   _____

5. **Buildings**

   _____
   _____
   _____

4 b) Fill in the following sentences with some of the words from **4 a)**.

1. We live in a large _____ outside of town.
2. We have to pay a high _____ for it.
3. The No. 67 _____ stops just opposite our house.
4. But we usually walk to the _____ to catch the train into town.
5. The _____ arrives at the station at 8 o'clock in the morning.
6. I work in a _____ where I sell a lot of stamps.
7. My flatmate works in a _____ where she sells TVs.
8. When we get home from work we have to _____ the flat.
9. She usually _____ and I do the washing-up.
10. There is another flat in the _____ of our house.

Exercise 5 · Everyday life

Translate the following sentences into English.

1. Ich interessiere mich für diese Wohnung.

2. Wie viele Zimmer hat die Wohnung?

3. Gibt es einen Parkplatz in der Nähe *(nearby)*?

4. Normalerweise mache ich den Abwasch.

5. Er räumt nie sein Zimmer auf.

6. Manchmal ärgert mich das.

7. Aber gewöhnlich komme ich gut mit ihm aus.

8. Wo arbeitest du?

9. Ich gehe zum Berufskolleg *(college)* in der Stadt.

10. Das Berufskolleggebäude ist neben dem Hauptbahnhof.

Unit 2 — Making choices

Exercise 1 · What course are they doing?

1 a) This is a tricky task for puzzle fans. There are 15 vocational courses hidden in the college building. Find the courses and mark them as in the example.
The words may be written horizontally →, vertically ↕, diagonally ↘ ↗ or backwards ←.

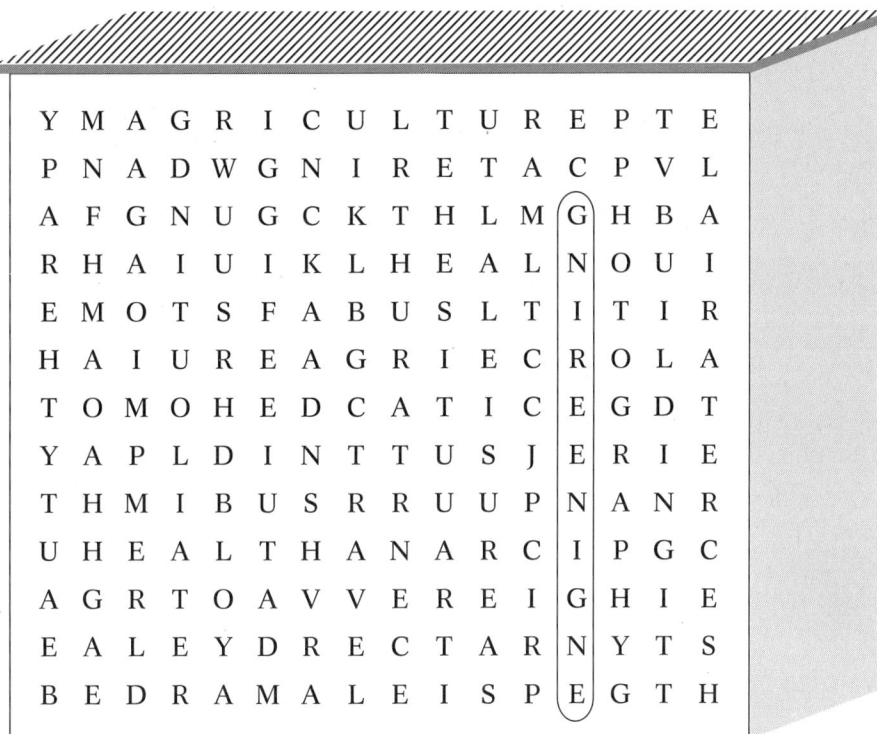

1 b) Complete the following sentences with a verb from the box in the Present Continuous and a suitable word from the puzzle above.

make	look at
cook	put (2x)
plant	draw
type	build

1. Pete _is making_ some tools, he is doing a course in _engineering_.
2. I _____ a meal, I am doing a course in _____.
3. Robin _____ a film in his camera, he is doing a course in _____.
4. Sarah and Kim _____ some holiday leaflets, they are doing a course in _____.
5. James _____ a letter, he is doing a _____ course.
6. I _____ some vegetables, I am doing a course in _____.
7. Jenny _____ a wall, she is doing a course in _____.
8. Simon _____ on some make-up, he is doing a course in _____.
9. Jake and I _____ a picture, we are doing a course in _____.

Exercise 2 · What are they doing?

2 a) Write the names of the objects below the pictures.

1. _____   2. _____   3. _____

4. _____   5. _____   6. _____

2 b) Now complete the following sentences to say what the people in the sentences are doing with these objects. Use the verbs and expressions in the boxes and keep the objects in the same order as in the pictures above.

| clean   travel   watch | in the kitchen   her teeth   to Canada |
| talk   ~~have~~   count | to each other   the money   TV |

1. Sarah and Robin _are having a cup of tea in the kitchen._
2. Sally _____.
3. Jake and I _____.
4. Simon and Jenny _____.
5. Andy _____.
6. Mark _____.

Exercise 3 · An interview with the Careers Officer

Put the verbs in brackets into the correct form – either Present Continuous or Present Simple.

CO So Mike, I want to start with your personal profile. I have your name and date of birth already. Now tell me, where (1) __do__ you __live__ (live)?

M   Well, at the moment I (2) __am still living__ (still live) with my parents, but I
    (3) _____ (not want) to stay there much longer.
    I (4) _____ (hope) to get a flat of my own soon.

10 ■ ten

CO I see, and what (5) _____ your father _____ (do)?
M   He's a plumber. He (6) _____ (work) for a firm in Birmingham.
CO And your mother?
M   Well, she (7) _____ (not work) at the moment.
    She (8) _____ (do) a training course in Travel and Tourism at the college.
CO That's interesting, why (9) _____ she _____ (do) that?
M   She says that now we (10) _____ (be) all over 16, she wants a new career.
CO Good. And what about you, Mike? What (11) _____ you _____ (want) to do?
M   Well, I (12) _____ (leave) school in a month and after that, well, I (13) _____ (not have) any plans.
CO (14) _____ you _____ (have) any special interests?
M   I (15) _____ (like) music and I (16) _____ (learn) to play the guitar at the moment.
CO That's nice, but of course, it (17) _____ (not be) easy to find a job in the music business. What about a college course?
M   I'm not sure. Of course my mother (18) _____ (enjoy) her course, but she (19) _____ (not earn) any money right now.
CO If you do a YT course you can combine work and study and they usually (20) _____ (give) some assistance towards the cost of lodgings.
M   (21) _____ they? That's good news. (22) _____ you _____ (think) I could still have my own flat then?
CO It's possible. Now why don't you take this leaflet with you? You can think about it and come and see me again.

Exercise 4 · The wrong word

In the following sentences the word which is underlined is used incorrectly.
Replace it with the correct word.

1. I have to train for three years to do this job, it's <u>unskilled</u> work.
   I have to train for three years to do this job, it's skilled work.

2. Of course, it's a big <u>advantage</u> if you don't have any qualifications.
   _____
   _____.

3. The Careers Officer can give you a lot of good <u>advise</u>.
   _____
   _____.

eleven ■ 11

2

4. An apprenticeship offers you <u>off-the-job</u> training.

5. I'm not very good at Maths, I'm afraid it's one of my <u>strengths.</u>

6. Nowadays there is so much <u>employment</u> that people find it difficult to get a job.

7. College is amazing, I'm <u>hating</u> every minute.

8. I'm doing a <u>part-time</u> course, it's from nine to four o'clock every day.

Exercise 5 · Back to college

Translate the following sentences into German.

1. Nowadays young people often don't want to go to college when they leave school.

2. They believe that college courses are a waste of time because even well-qualified people are unemployed today.

3. But Careers Officers try to persuade them that this is not always true.

4. They tell students that college life can be fun and that the courses are interesting.

5. Students who decide to go to college agree with the Careers Officers.

Exercise 6 · Interviewing a flatmate

Translate the following sentences into English.

1. Wo wohnst du zur Zeit?
   _____?

2. Ich wohne im Moment bei einer Freundin.
   _____.

3. Ich bin das aber leid, weil ich kein eigenes Zimmer habe.
   _____.

4. Und was machst du?
   _____?

5. Ich studiere zur Zeit Wirtschaftslehre; ich glaube, jeder braucht heutzutage Qualifikationen.
   _____.

6. Ja, das stimmt. Und was machst du in deiner Freizeit?
   _____?

7. Ich mache regelmäßig Sport, damit ich gesund bleibe.
   _____.

8. Und wie ist es mit deinen Essgewohnheiten?
   _____?

9. Ich koche gern und ich verbringe viel Zeit in der Küche.
   _____.

10. Ich mache zur Zeit sogar einen Kochkurs im College.
    _____.

Unit 3 Working lives

Exercise 1 · What's their job?

1 a) Look at the following people and write the names of their jobs under the pictures.

Louise

◀ 1. _landlady_____
   2. _____ ▶

Julian

Janet

Tanja

3. _____   4. _____

John and Debbie

◀ 5. _____
   6. _____ ▶

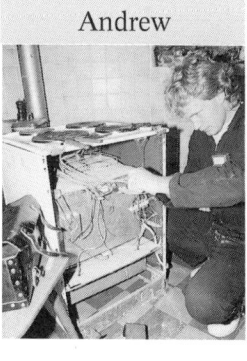
Andrew

Joe

Frank

7. _____   8. _____

1 b) Match the jobs from **1 a)** with the letters for the correct words in the boxes.

Job	1	2	3	4	5	6	7	8
Verb	E							
Noun	Z							

A install   Z flats and rooms
B cut   Y clothes
C design   X planes
D repair   W other people's hair
E let   V houses
F fix   U toilets
G sell   T electrical equipment
H build   S cars

14 ■ fourteen

1 c) Make two sentences about the people and their jobs.
Write down the jobs and what the people do in their jobs.
Use the words from **1 a)** and **b)**.

1. *Louise is a landlady. She lets flats and rooms.*
2. _____
3. _____
4. _____
5. _____
6. _____
7. _____
8. _____

Exercise 2 · Sally's life

2 a) Fill in the Past Simple of the following verbs.

1. be (am/are/is) __was/were__
2. become _____
3. know _____
4. go _____
5. try _____
6. think _____
7. have _____
8. take _____
9. leave _____
10. feel _____
11. do _____

2 b) Find a suitable verb in the above list and complete the following text about Sally.
Be careful – some sentences are negative!

When Sally (1) __was__ twelve years old she (2) _____ to an audition. She (3) _____ to get the part of Carrie in 'Southfields'. She (4) (not) _____ anything about acting at that time but she (5) _____ that it could be great fun. Sally (6) _____ very nervous in the beginning and she (7) _____ to learn a lot. So she (8) _____ some training lessons. Sally (9) (not) _____ well at school. At the age of 16 she (10) _____ school and (11) _____ independent.

fifteen ■ 15

Exercise 3 · A success story

This is Tim Ryan.

And here is some information about him.

1. go – school 1975–1987
2. pass – exams 1987
3. work – bank 1987–1989
4. become – musician 1989
5. make – first single 1990
6. record – first hit single in England 1993
7. have – own group 1995–1997
8. become – music producer 1997

Where?
When?
What?

Ask Tim Ryan questions (Q) about his life and answer them (A) in the Past Simple.
Use the question words above.

1. Q *When did you go to school?*
   A *I went to* _____.

2. Q _____?
   A _____.

3. Q _____?
   A _____.

4. Q _____?
   A _____.

5. Q _____?
   A _____.

6. Q _____?
   A _____.

7. Q _____?
   A _____.

8. Q _____?
   A _____.

Exercise 4 · Do you remember?

Across →

1. schauspielern, spielen
2. Schauspielerin
4. Stimme
5. dumm
7. Rolle
10. Entwicklung
15. vorschlagen
16. verbringen, ausgeben

Down ↓

1. Vorsprechen, Vorsingen
3. dünn
4. Zuschauer/in
6. üben
8. sich in Verbindung setzen mit
9. (sich) verbessern
11. Ärger, Schwierigkeiten
12. besorgt
13. stolz
14. erwarten

Exercise 5 · Schoolgirl soap star

The following text is part of the interview with Sally Black. Translate it into German.

(1) I'd like to play different roles, of course, but soaps have one big advantage. (2) We're able to discuss the development of the characters with the scriptwriter. (3) For example, I suggested that Carrie could become anorexic. (4) Too many girls are trying to be as thin as the models they see in magazines. (5) I thought we could show them how dangerous this can be.

1. _____
_____.
2. _____
_____.
3. _____
_____.
4. _____
_____.
5. _____
_____.

Exercise 6 · An interview with a film star

Translate the following sentences into English.

1. Wann haben Sie die Schule verlassen?

2. Ich habe die Schule verlassen, als ich sechzehn Jahre alt war.

3. Was haben Sie dann gemacht?

4. Zuerst habe ich eine Arbeit als Verkäuferin begonnen.

5. Wo haben Sie gearbeitet?

6. Ich habe ein Jahr lang in einem Schuhgeschäft gearbeitet.

7. Und was geschah dann?

8. Ich traf eine Schulfreundin. Sie war Schauspielerin in einer Seifenoper.

9. Hat Ihnen Ihre Freundin geholfen?

10. Ja. Ich mochte meine Arbeit nicht und ich dachte, dass diese Gelegenheit zu gut war, um sie auszulassen. So bekam ich meine erste Rolle in ‚Gute Freunde, schlechte Freunde'.

Unit 4 Healthy eating

Exercise 1 · What kind of food is it?

1 a) We can divide the food we eat into different groups:
meat, fruit, dairy products (*Milchprodukte*), cereals (*Getreideprodukte*) and drinks.
Write the names of the foods in the box below under the correct heading.

> ~~bacon~~   bananas   bread   muesli   sausages   coffee
> hamburger   yoghurt   baguette   strawberries   butter   water
> tea   cornflakes   cheese   apples   beer   milk   orange   wine

Meat	Fruit	Dairy products	Cereals	Drinks
bacon				

1 b) Now complete the following sentences with one of
the food items above and one of the adjectives in the box.

> lovely   delicious   fatty
> disgusting   healthy   ~~strong~~   dry

1. I can't drink this ____*tea*____, it's too ____*strong*____.
2. These nice red _____ are really fresh, they taste _____.
3. Ugh! I can't eat this piece of _____, it's too _____.
4. Have one of these _____, it'll do you good, it's very _____.
5. Have a piece of this_____, it's _____ and sweet.
6. You shouldn't fry that _____ in so much oil, it's already really _____.
7. I don't like cold _____ for breakfast, they're _____.

4

Exercise 2 · Comparing

2 a) Fill in the missing forms.

1. cold	colder	coldest
2. warm		
3.	nicer	
4. weak		
5.		slimmest
6.	noisier	
7.		best
8. healthy		
9.	worse	
10. hot		
11.		cheapest
12. tasty		

2 b) Now compare the following.
Rewrite the sentences, using one of the words in the table above.

1. Coffee isn't as healthy as fruit juice.
   Fruit juice is healthier than coffee.

2. Nothing I have ever eaten is as bad as this soup.
   This is the _____ **soup I have ever eaten.**

3. Nobody I know makes as much noise as you do, Gillian.
   _____.

4. I have never eaten such a nice meal.
   _____.

5. These apples are quite cheap – 85p per pound, those ones there are 93p per pound.
   _____.

6. Lizzie isn't as slim as Sue.
   _____.

7. Nobody I know is such a good dancer as Jane.
   _____.

8. A piece of dry toast is not as tasty as grilled bacon on toast.
   _____
   _____.

Exercise 3 · Describing people

3 a) Look at the photos of the two people below, then choose suitable adjectives from the box to describe them.

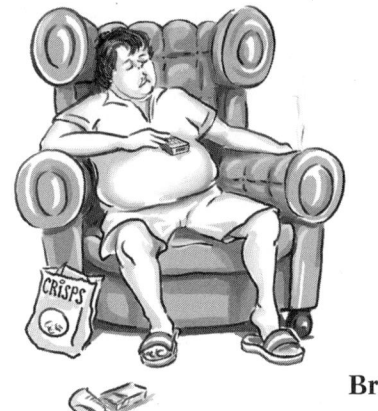

Brian

Kevin

```
short    lazy     weak    young
plain    healthy  fat     awake
strong   fit      asleep  old
attractive  slim  tall    unhealthy
```

1. *short*
2. _____
3. _____
4. _____
5. _____
6. _____
7. _____
8. _____
9. _____
10. _____
11. _____
12. _____
13. _____
14. _____
15. _____
16. _____

3 b) Fill in the gaps in these sentences with a suitable word from either the box above or the box below.

```
medium-height    medium-sized
middle-aged      reasonable
```

Janet is not tall or short, she is (1) *medium-height*. She has dark hair and eyes. She isn't too fat or too thin, she's (2) _____. She does a lot of sport so she is quite (3) _____. A lot of people think she's very (4) _____ to look at. She's only 19 years old so she's still quite (5) _____. She goes to a fitness studio regularly twice a week so she's really (6) _____. She also rides a motorbike which is (7) _____ but still okay. At the moment she is telephoning a friend and feeling very (8) _____. It's hard work for her to keep in such good shape.

Exercise 4 · The Elvis test

Are you an Elvis expert yet? Put the letters of the words in the box into the right order and then fill in the gaps below.

> obcan threkareba lerquris curtk verrid
> mlupp gintea ascrolie thare katact

1. '_Heartbreak_ Hotel' was his first world-wide hit record.
2. A small animal which Elvis used to eat: _____
3. Elvis' favourite snack included this food: _____
4. A job Elvis did before he became King of Rock 'n Roll (two words): _____
5. His mother wasn't fat or thin, she was _____.
6. In Elvis' later years it was his only pleasure: _____
7. At the end of his life, Elvis consumed 100,000 of these every day: _____
8. Elvis died as a result of this (two words): _____

Exercise 5 · Lizzie's life

Fill in the gaps in the following text with the correct form of the adjective in the box. Use each word once.

> delicious pleasant disgusting beautiful
> interesting comfortable attractive

Although Lizzie is not the most (1) _____ girl in the world, she is certainly very (2) _____. She eats very healthy food which she says tastes (3) _____ than junk food. She thinks that fatty food and especially cold sausages and chips are the (4) _____ things you could possibly eat for breakfast. She shares a very (5) _____ flat with Sue and Jane. She finds that sharing a flat is much (6) _____ than living on your own, especially when the people you share with are as (7) _____ as Sue and Jane.

Exercise 6 · Eating out

Translate the following sentences into English.

1. ‚Rosina's' ist eins der nettesten *(pleasant)* Restaurants hier in der Stadt.

2. Die Gerichte sind alle sehr gesund und schmecken wirklich lecker.

3. Es ist sehr beliebt, obwohl es teurer ist als andere Restaurants.

4. Eins der leckersten Gerichte ist Pfannkuchen mit Erdbeeren, Sahne und Sirup.

5. Die Kellner sind freundlicher und höflicher als in anderen Restaurants.

6. Wenn du nicht viel essen willst oder nicht zunehmen willst *(put on weight)*, haben sie einige interessante Kleinigkeiten *(snacks)*.

Unit 5 — Healthy living

Exercise 1 · The parts of the body

1 a) Put the following parts of the body in the right order from top to toe.

> ~~head~~ waist leg foot
> hip shoulder neck
> ankle toe chest

1. _head_
2. _____
3. _____
4. _____
5. _____
6. _____
7. _____
8. _____
9. _____
10. _____

1 b) In the chart below, fill in all the parts of the body which belong to the arm. Then make pairs with the parts which belong to the leg.

> knee toe shoulder
> ankle wrist hip finger
> hand foot elbow

arm	leg

24 ■ twenty-four

Exercise 2 · Doctor's advice

2 a) Read what advice the doctor may give you when you feel ill.

1. You shouldn't go to school.
2. You should stay at home.
3. You shouldn't get out of bed too soon.
4. You should take your tablets regularly.
5. You should drink a lot.

Rewrite the above sentences. Use the imperative.

1. Don't go to school.
2. _____.
3. _____.
4. _____.
5. _____.

2 b) Read the doctor's advice on how to take your medicine.

1. Take two tablets three times a day.
2. Don't take them before your meals.
3. Drink half a glass of water with the tablets.
4. Don't drink any alcohol at the same time.
5. Keep medicine away from little children.

Now give the doctor's advice with *should* or *shouldn't*.

1. You should take two tablets three times a day.
2. _____.
3. _____.
4. _____.
5. _____.

PARAPRIN

For headaches, toothache, colds and sore throats.

Dose: Adults 1 – 3 tablets daily or every 2 or 3 hours.

Soluble Pain Relief

Rennoes

Digestive **Rennoes** Tablets

For troubled stomachs.
Take two Rennoes after meals.

5

Exercise 3 · Watch your health!

3 a) The following twelve pictures tell you something about how to keep fit and healthy. Decide which things people should use, do, eat or drink <u>less</u> and mark them with a pen as in the example.

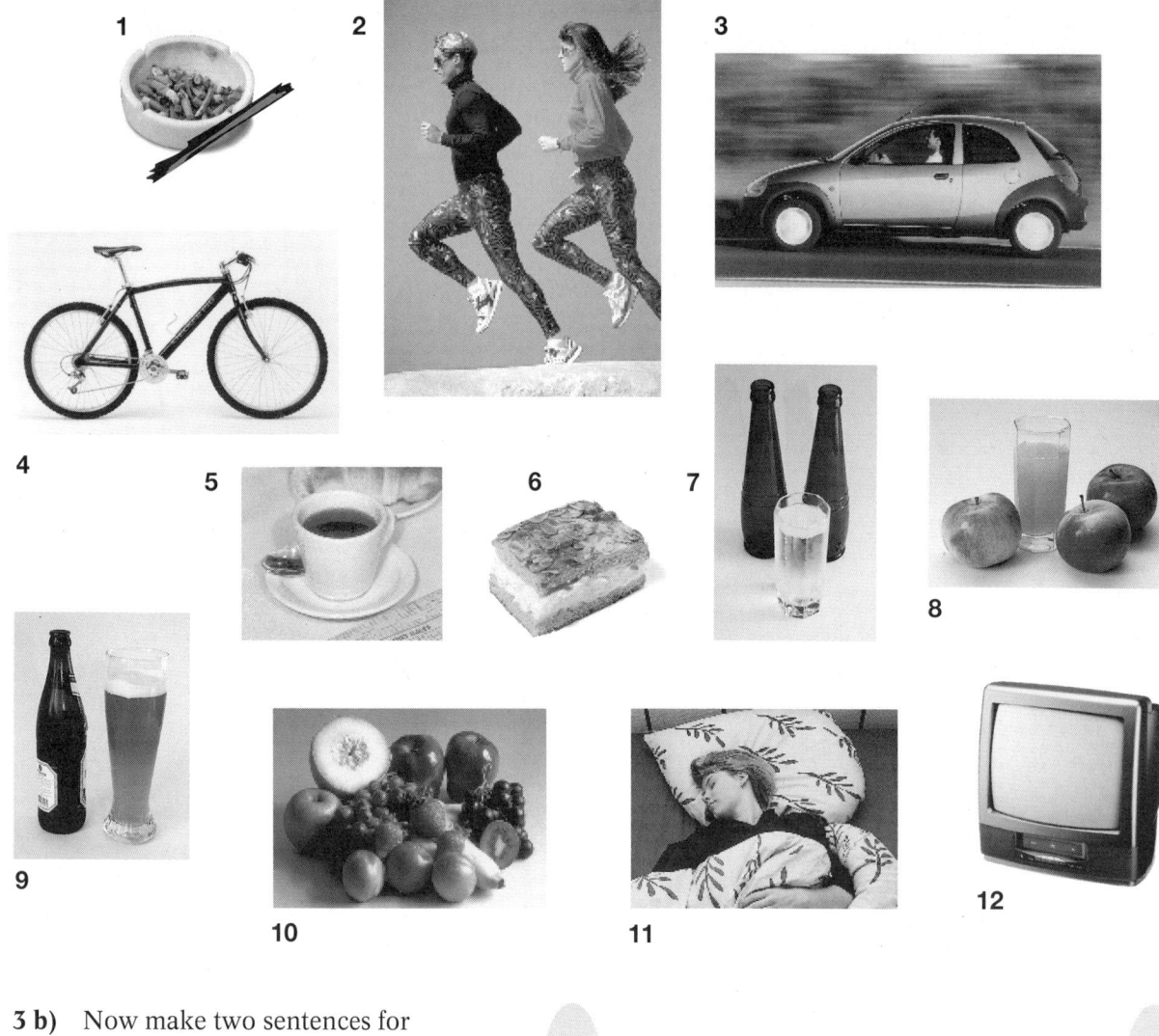

3 b) Now make two sentences for each picture to give tips on how to keep fit and healthy. The words on the right will help you.

you should   you shouldn't   do   don't
more   less   too much   so much

should / shouldn't

1. You shouldn't smoke so much.
2. You should do more sports.
3. _____.
4. _____.
5. _____.

26 ■ *twenty-six*

6. _____.
7. _____.
8. _____.
9. _____.
10. _____.
11. _____.
12. _____.

do / don't

1. *Don't smoke so much.* _____
2. _____.
3. _____.
4. _____.
5. _____.
6. _____.
7. _____.
8. _____.
9. _____.
10. _____.
11. _____.
12. _____.

Exercise 4 · Activities

4 a) Find the names of the sports in the pictures and write them in the list below a suitable heading. Use the syllables for help.

nis – ing – ket – cy – ball – golf – vol – danc – ming – ball – ley – ~~foot~~ – ten – cling – swim – bas – ~~ball~~

play	go
football	

twenty-seven ■ 27

4 b)

Your friend wants to do some sport together with you. Choose the right sport for him / her and give him / her a tip. Use *Let's ...* or *Why don't we ...?* to start.

1. I've got an old racket at home.
2. I like water.
3. I enjoy the open air.
4. I like music.

1. Let's play tennis. / Why don't we play tennis?
2. _____
3. _____
4. _____

Exercise 5 · Spelling

In many English words you find pairs of vowels (a, e, i, o, u), for example in: "My h**ea**rt is b**ea**ting". In the following exercise you will find words from Unit 5 in which two vowels are missing. Complete the words.

1. bl_ee_d
2. br___the
3. pat___nt
4. r___se
5. m___nt___n
6. coff___
7. t___ busy
8. h___lthy
9. wh___l
10. br___kfast
11. m___l
12. k___p
13. he g___s
14. h___vy
15. he d___sn't
16. kn___
17. thr___t
18. w___st
19. ___robics
20. w___ght-lifting

Exercise 6 · First Aid

Translate the following sentences into English.

1. Bewege den Patienten nicht. _____.

2. Untersuche ihn von Kopf bis Fuß (Zeh).
   _____.

3. Wenn der Patient bei Bewusstsein ist, rede mit ihm.
   _____.

4. Wenn du dem Patienten nicht helfen kannst, rufe sofort Hilfe herbei.
   _____.

5. Du solltest über Erste Hilfe Bescheid wissen, damit du anderen Menschen helfen kannst.
   _____
   _____.

Unit 6 Fact or fiction?

Exercise 1 · What were these people doing?

Write complete sentences from the following prompts.
Use the correct Past Tense (Past Continuous and Past Simple).

1. Tim / wait at the bus stop / start to rain
   Tim was waiting at the bus stop when it started to rain.

2. Ann / look at the advertisements / the phone ring

3. The Jones / watch a soap opera / hear a call for help

4. I / wait at the airport / they / call out the flight number

5. We / go to college / see an accident

6. I / work on the computer / the electricity go off

7. My boss / wait at the traffic lights / his case drop to the ground

8. The students / do a test / a bird fly into the room

9. Joan / stand in the bank / the bank robber come in

10. We / have an English lesson / a helicopter land outside

Exercise 2 · What happened then?

What did the people in Exercise **1** do afterwards? The words in the box will help you.

> scream   stop writing
> ~~put up his umbrella~~   sit in the dark
> look out of the windows
> all his papers fall out   go to Gate 7
> phone for an ambulance
> switch off the TV   put down the magazine

1. *When it started to rain he put up his umbrella.*
2. *When the phone rang she* _____.
3. _____.
4. _____.
5. _____.
6. _____.
7. _____.
8. _____.
9. _____.
10. _____.

Exercise 3
A crossword puzzle

1 Feuerwehrmann
2 Metallbehälter, -tank
3 Waldbrand
4 Taucher
5 kämpfen
6 Schlauch
7 verbrannt
8 Hubschrauber
9 Geschichte
10 Notfall

4 D I V E R

Exercise 4 · Mind maps

Look at the four texts in Exercise **6** in the Student's Book, then complete the following mind maps with some of the words from the texts.

m_____   g_____
                              POLITICS ── politician
i_____   l_____   P_____   e_____ M_____   r_____

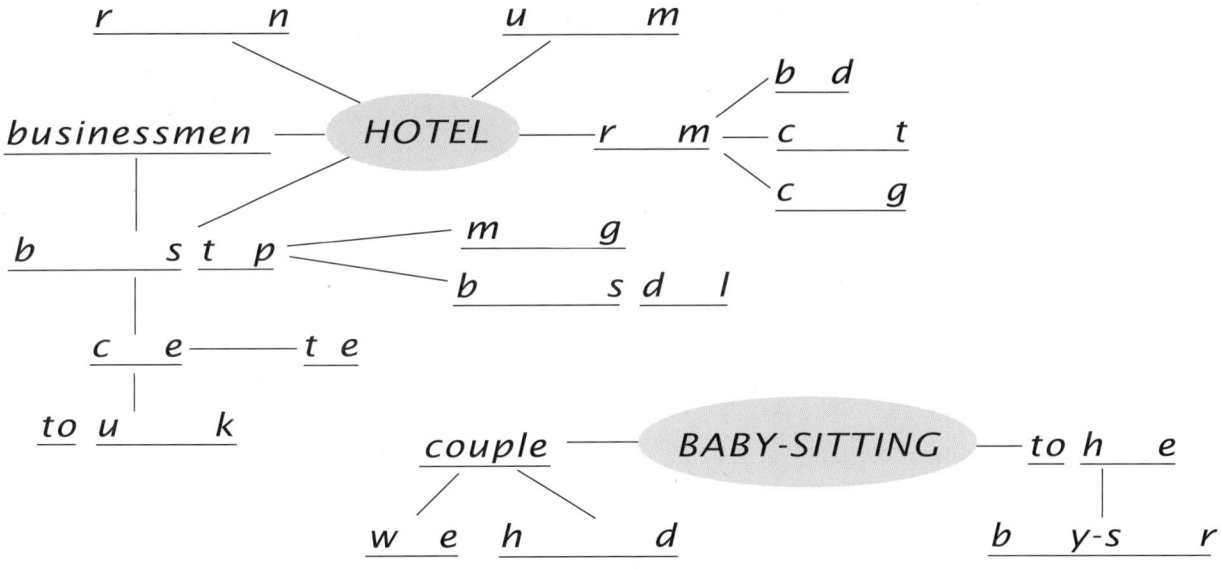

Exercise 5 · A strange story

Translate the following sentences into English.

1. Ich sprach letzte Woche mit einem alten Klassenkameraden.

2. Er erzählte mir eine seltsame Geschichte.

3. Während er zu Mittag aß, rief seine Frau an.

4. Sie sagte ihm, dass sie sich in einem alten Hotel in England aufhielt.

5. Sie erzählte, dass sie gestern abend im Bett lag, als jemand an die Tür klopfte.

6. Als sie die Tür aufmachte, stand dort eine Frau im Schlafanzug.

7. Diese Frau erzählte, dass sie keinen Schlüssel zu ihrem Zimmer dabei hatte.

8. Die Frau meines Bekannten fragte sie, warum sie nur einen Schlafanzug trug.

9. Sie antwortete, dass sie schlafwandelte (*sleepwalked*).

10. Sie hatte sich ausgeschlossen (*locked out*).

Unit 7 — Looking ahead

Exercise 1 · Odd one out

1 a) In each of the following groups of words, find the word which doesn't belong there and cross it out.

1. crystal ball – ~~satellite dish~~ – tea-leaves – horoscope – palm of the hand
2. weather forecast – traffic report – news headlines – chimney – advert
3. cloudy – windy – wet – murder – temperature
4. vehicles – calm – cross – worried – careful
5. charge – roof – admit – deny – court

1 b) Now give your reasons for choosing each word.

1. A satellite dish has nothing to do with horoscopes.
2. _____.
3. _____.
4. _____.
5. _____.

1 c) Choose the correct word from each of the groups above to complete these sentences.

1. My mother read my _____ to me from the paper.
2. I heard the _____ on the radio this morning. It said that City Road was closed.
3. Look how _____ it is, it'll probably rain later.
4. Sam's mother is _____ that he won't succeed in his examination because he hasn't done any work.
5. My friend had to go to _____ last week for driving too fast down the High Street.

1 d) Find the opposites of the following words.

1. admit   – _____
2. warm   – _____
3. reality – _____
4. past   – _____

Exercise 2 · Life in the future

Look at these pictures of life in the future. Make a sentence for each picture to say what will happen. The words in the box will help you.

1

2

3

4

Britain	be	a black Prime Minister
~~Most people~~	have	~~by bike~~
Everybody	~~travel~~	a video telephone
Every home	have	by credit card
There	pay	smaller
Cars	be	more free time
Most people	have	houses with solar energy heating

7

6

5

1. _Most people will travel by bike._
2. _____
3. _____
4. _____
5. _____
6. _____
7. _____

Exercise 3 · Horoscopes

Join the words in the box to make predictions similar to the ones in the Student's Book.

~~Aquarius~~	~~argue~~	~~happy~~
Pisces	not easy	become better
Aries	love life	money
Taurus	happy	work situation
Gemini	journey	work
Cancer	boring	improve
Leo	new friend	be careful
Virgo	winner	money
Libra	boring	nothing special
Scorpio	success	take it easy
Sagittarius	decide	effect
Capricorn	improve	decision

1. Aquarius – You will argue with a friend but by April you will be happy again.
2.
3.
4.
5.
6.
7.
8.
9.
10.
11.
12.

Exercise 4 · Advice from a fortune teller

4 a) Lizzie has gone to a fortune teller. Here are some of the things the fortune teller says. Complete the sentences using either *can*, *can't*, *must* or *needn't* or their alternative forms *(not) be able to* or *(not) have to*.

1. At the moment life looks difficult for you and you ___can't / aren't able to___ see how it may improve.
2. But you _____ worry about succeeding in your examination, you have worked very hard.
3. However, a friend of yours may be unlucky at the moment, so he _____ be careful if he has a dangerous job.
4. But he _____ be sure that nothing serious will happen to him.

4 b) Later Matt went to see the fortune teller, too. Make complete sentences from the prompts below and a suitable future form of either *(not) be able to* or *(not) have to*.

1. work harder / or lose your job
   You will have to work harder or you will lose your job.

2. save your money / or not have enough for your holiday in Greece
   _____

3. forget your problems in Greece / because be beautiful there
   _____

4. get up early / because be on holiday
   _____

5. speak Greek / many people understand English
   _____

6. lie on the beach every day / be so sunny
   _____

7. but show your suntan to your friends at home / weather be too cold there
   _____

8. worry about work at all soon / win lottery next year
   _____

Exercise 5 · The news

Translate these sentences into English.

1. Wissenschaftler sagen, dass es bald ein Heilmittel *(cure)* gegen Aids geben wird.

2. Der neue britische Premierminister wird morgen in Bonn eintreffen.

3. Zukünftig werden junge Leute mit 16 den Führerschein machen können.

4. Zwei Männer werden morgen vor Gericht erscheinen.

5. Wegen Straßenbauarbeiten *(road works)* wird die Polizei River Street heute nachmittag schließen.

6. Es wird eine Umleitung über Bank Street geben.

7. Die Gruppe ‚Flash' wird am Samstag ein Konzert im Hyde Park geben.

8. Die Gruppe wird den Erlös *(profits)* des Konzerts für Aids-Patienten spenden *(give)*.

9. Das Wetter wird morgen kalt und nass sein.

10. Die Temperaturen werden zwischen 6 und 10 Grad Celsius sein.

Unit 8 · Making plans

Exercise 1 · What are these people going to do?

Describe the situations in the pictures in complete sentences. The verbs in the box will help you.

1. hotel guest
2. businessman 
3. business woman 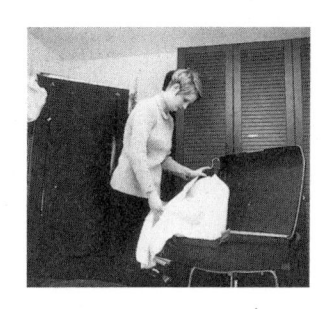
4. customer 
5. customer 
6. employer 
7. nurse 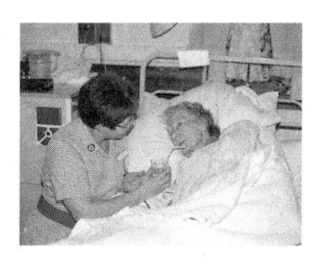
8. guest 

| buy | offer | ~~go~~ | give | get | travel | meet | have |

1. *The hotel guest is going to go to her room.*
2. _____ .
3. _____ .
4. _____ .
5. _____ .
6. _____ .
7. _____ .
8. _____ .

thirty-seven ■ 37

Exercise 2 · Young people only!

Look at page 50 in the Student's Book and fill in suitable prepositions from the box.

after	at (2x)	between
by	for	in (2x)	near
of	on	round	to (2x)

Cheap 48-hour tickets
(1) _____ *all young people*
(2) _____ *15 and 25!*

- Take a trip (3) _____ Edinburgh or (4) _____ Scotland.
- Stay (5) _____ the heart (6) _____ the Highlands, camp (7) _____ Loch Ness.
- Go (8) _____ your local railway station right now!
- You can travel (9) _____ coach or train and stay (10) _____ guesthouses or hostels.
- If you travel (11) _____ 9.30, or (12) _____ the weekends and (13) _____ public holidays, you pay half the price.
- So: Buy your ticket (14) _____ your station now!

Exercise 3 · Can you help?

Ask for help in a polite way.
Use *Could*, *Would* or *Can* to start your questions.

Could you ..., please?
Would you ..., please?
Can you ..., please?

1. (I have to make a phone call home.)
2. (I'd like to write a postcard to my friend.)
3. (This fast food doesn't taste nice.)
4. (We don't know how to get to the youth hostel.)
5. (I'd like to look at the travel ads.)

1. (lend / phonecard) Could / Would / Can you lend me your phonecard, please?
2. (give / pen) _____?
3. (pass / ketchup) _____?
4. (show / way) _____?
5. (hand / newspaper) _____?

6. *Please remember us when you are in the U.S.* 6. (send / picture postcard) _____
_____?

7. *Lizzie, we want to buy some food.* 7. (lend / money) _____
_____?

8. *My fruit juice is warm.* 8. (bring / some ice) _____
_____?

Exercise 4 · A trip to Scotland

Translate these sentences into English.

1. Elaine und Steve planen eine Reise nach Schottland.

2. Sie haben sich bereits ihre Fahrkarten gekauft.

3. Gestern hat Steve Zimmer mit Frühstück für einige Nächte gebucht.

4. Steve und Elaine werden zuerst drei Tage in Edinburgh verbringen.

5. Elaine hat einen Reiseführer von Edinburgh gekauft und liest ihn gerade.

6. Sie wird Steve die Sehenswürdigkeiten *(sights)* der Stadt zeigen.

7. Dann werden sie eine Woche in der Nähe von Loch Ness bleiben.

8. Ihr Urlaub wird wahrscheinlich sehr schön.

Exercise 5 · A crossword puzzle

Across →

2 A document with your name and photo which you have to show when you enter or leave a country
6 It keeps you out of the house because the doors are closed and you do not have a key.
10 A large house where people can stay cheaply for a short time
12 A shopkeeper who sells newspapers and magazines
14 The room you use for cooking
15 A piece of paper that you must fill in if you want to get e. g. a railcard (Two words)
17 Twelve o'clock at night
22 The place to which you are going
23 You can have it or use it and you do not have to pay for it. It is …
24 A shopkeeper who sells cigarettes and tobacco

Down ↓

1 A large, comfortable bus that carries people on long journeys
3 If you have it in your bathroom, you wash yourself by standing under a spray of water from above
4 A field where you play football or cricket
5 It does not cost very much. It is …
7 It states that people must stay inside the house after a particular time at night.
8 It is a small hotel.(Two words)
9 The money you pay for a journey
11 A railway system in which electric trains travel below the ground in tunnels
13 A building where trains stop
16 A journey you make to a place and back again
17 The food you eat at lunchtime or in the evening
18 The time when people do not go to work or to school
19 The amount of money you have to pay to buy something
20 It is a book that gives tourists information – or a person who shows tourists around places of interest.
21 A piece of paper which shows that you have paid for a journey

8

forty-one ■ 41

Unit 9 — Making arrangements

Exercise 1 · Word fields

1 a) Choose words and expressions from the box to add to the word fields.

> dishonest   guests   arrangements
> hurtful   invite   excuse   cooking
> coward   tell the truth   welcome

(word field: dinner party)

(word field: liar)

1 b) Now use the main words above with one of the others in the word field to make sentences.

dinner party

1. *I have made the arrangements for my dinner party.*
2. _____ .

liar

3. _____ .
4. _____ .

1 c) Complete the sentences using one other word or expression from the fields above.

1. I'm having a dinner party, but I haven't asked the _____ yet.
2. She's not really a liar, but she sometimes doesn't _____ .

Exercise 2 · A busy week

Mon	go to cinema with Tom
Tue	meet Pam for tea
Wed	a.m. play tennis Sally p.m. cook supper Matt
Thur	visit grandmother
Fri	go to Nick's birthday party
Sat	spend weekend
Sun	in Hamburg

Complete the conversation below using the information from the diary.

Pete Would you like to come to a film with me on Monday, Jane?
Jane Sorry, Pete. I can't. (1) *I'm going to the cinema with Tom on Monday.*
Pete Well, what about Tuesday?
Jane On Tuesday (2) _____.
Pete Have you got time on Wednesday then?
Jane No, let me see, ... in the morning (3) _____ and in the evening (4) _____.
Pete You really are busy next week, aren't you? Any chance of meeting on Thursday?
Jane No, I'm afraid (5) _____ on Thursday.
Pete Friday then?
Jane Sorry, (6) _____.
Pete How about the weekend?
Jane Well no, (7) _____.
 I'm really sorry – but I'll phone you next week.

Exercise 3 · What happens next?

Make sentences from the information given to show what is going to happen.

1. Adrian has picked up the phone and dialled Pandora's number. (invite to a party)
   He's going to invite her to a party.

2. Pandora has taken a bath and put on her best dress. (meet Nigel)
   She's going to _____.

3. Sabre is growling at Adrian and showing his teeth. (bite)
   _____.

4. Adrian's mother has gone into the kitchen and is cutting up some vegetables. (cook lunch)
   _____.

5. Adrian's father has got out his tools and is looking at the car. (repair)

_____.

6. Bert Baxter has got out the dog food and has called Sabre. (feed)

_____.

7. Adrian has picked up the hedge cutters and gone into the garden. (cut)

_____.

8. Pandora and Nigel have bought tickets for the cinema. (see a film)

_____.

Exercise 4 · A telephone call

Pete has phoned Jane again. Complete their conversation using *should*, *might* or *would like*.

Pete   Hi Jane, how was your weekend?

Jane   Oh, it was very hectic. I'm so tired now. I really (1) *should* learn to do less.

Pete   But I hope you'll have some spare time this week. I (2) _____ to take you to a film.

Jane   That's very kind of you, Pete, I (3) _____ have some time at the weekend, but I'm not quite sure yet.

Pete   Well, that sounds good! Friday or Saturday then.

Jane   Well, not Friday – the flat's a terrible mess. I really (4) _____ clean it up a bit. My mother's coming next week and I (5) _____ to show her that I can be tidy.

Pete   I know what you mean. I (6) _____ even do some housework myself this week. Shall we say Saturday then?

Jane   O.K. Pete. There's that new Clint Eastwood film on and I (7) _____ to see it very much.

Exercise 5 · A dinner party

Translate the following sentences into English.

1. Möchtest du noch Kartoffeln, Jane? _____?

2. Nein danke, ich fange morgen mit meiner Diät an und ich sollte heute nicht so viel essen.

_____

_____.

3. Okay. Wenn du nichts mehr essen willst, werde ich die Teller in die Küche tragen.

_____

_____.

4. Brauchst du Hilfe, Lizzie?

_____?

5. Ja. Ich werde uns nachher einen Kaffee machen.

_____.

6. Gut; dann werde ich mit Matt reden. Er hat versprochen mir von seinem Urlaub zu erzählen.

_____

_____.

Exercise 6 · Another crossword puzzle

Across →

- 4 A young person who comes home to an empty house (Two words)
- 7 Pandora has decided to … out with Nigel.
- 8 Bert Baxter is an old-age …
- 10 The opposite of late
- 12 The colour of Pandora's hair
- 13 What you do with 12 across
- 14 You should put this down if you want to stop someone doing something.
- 17 Adrian's mother drinks … much at Christmas.
- 19 If you eat too many of these your skin is ruined.
- 20 When you've had enough of something you're … (Two words)

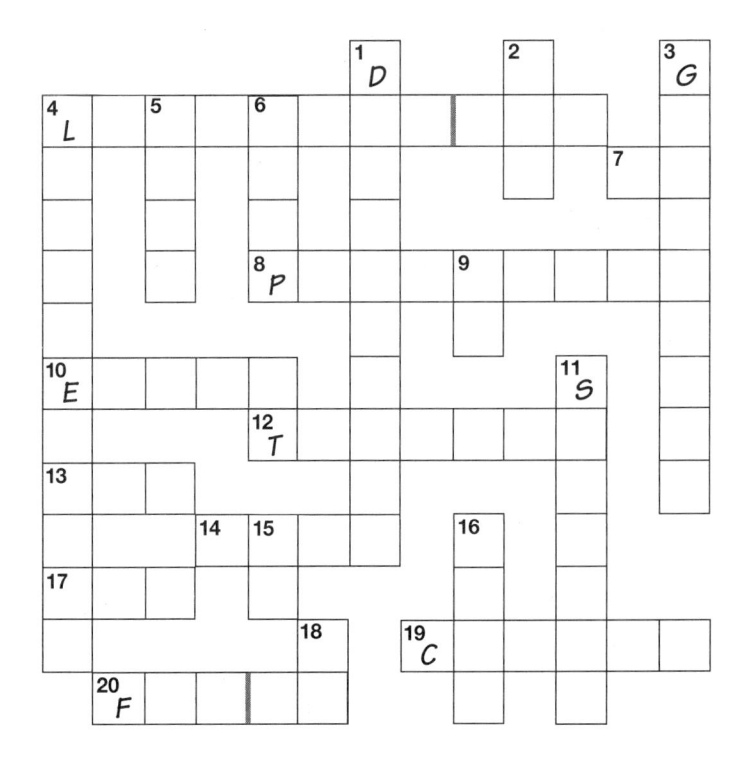

Down ↓

- 1 A young person who does criminal things
- 2 The … end on Adrian's father's car is broken.
- 3 A subject in school which teaches you about the earth
- 4 You take your clothes there to wash them.
- 5 Adrian's mother is learning to do this.
- 6 Samaritans … people in the area.
- 9 Adrian is … love with Pandora.
- 11 When you only think about yourself you are …
- 15 Adrian's mother starts work … Monday.
- 16 The temperature in the launderette
- 18 If Adrian goes to bed early on Thursday, he might get … early on Friday.

Unit 10 Superstitions and customs

Exercise 1 · What will happen if …?

1 a) Match the parts on the left with the ones on the right.

1. if/a black cat/cross/your path	A if/you/break a mirror
2. something/fall/on your head	B they/not/have/any children
3. you/have/seven years bad luck	C you/have/bad luck that day
4. if/a girl/catch/the bride's bouquet	D she/have/bad luck
5. if/someone/knock on wood/three times	E if/they/get married/in June
6. if/the bride and groom/not/cut/the wedding cake/first	F if you/walk/under a ladder
7. if/the bride/lose/her wedding ring	G she/be/the next bride
8. people/have/a happy marriage	H he/have/good luck

1	2	3	4	5	6	7	8
C							

1 b) Now write the complete sentences.

1. *If a black cat crosses your path, you will have bad luck that day.*
2. *Something will fall*
3.
4.
5.
6.
7.
8.

Exercise 2
At the wedding

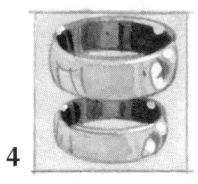

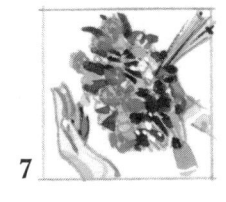

Look at the pictures.
Then fill in the right words. →

10 down is the holiday
after the wedding.

Exercise 3 · Getting married

3 a) Find phrases in the box which go with the verbs given.
Refer to the text on page 60 in the Student's Book.

1. invite *guests* _____
2. ask _____
3. buy _____
4. go to _____
5. take part _____
6. cut _____
7. go off _____
8. throw _____
9. return _____
10. carry _____

> a friend to be best man
> across the threshold
> ~~guests~~   home
> in the reception
> on honeymoon   the rings
> her bouquet of flowers
> the church to get married
> the wedding cake

forty-seven ■ 47

3 b) Now describe in complete sentences what the bride and groom do when they get married. Keep to the order of the words on page 47.

First the bride and groom invite their guests.

Then the groom _____
and _____.
On the wedding day _____
_____.
Afterwards _____
where _____.
Before _____
_____.
When _____
_____.

Exercise 4 · A critical situation

One evening a young man is on his way from London to Edinburgh in order to get married the next morning. Suddenly his car has a puncture.
He needs help because he hasn't got a jack. He is only half a mile away from the next garage. He can see a light there and hopes to find help.
But maybe they will close very soon …

1. not run to the garage
2. they close
3. not help him
4. not be able to drive his car
5. not get to Edinburgh on time
6. too late at the church
7. miss his wedding
8. the bride be angry
9. the bride not want to marry him any more – young man be free again

Now make a chain of sentences as in the examples.

1. *If the young man does not run to the garage, they will close.*
2. *If they close, they will not help him.*
3. *If they do not help him,* _____
_____.
4. _____
_____.

5. _____

6. _____

7. _____

8. _____

9. _____

10. *Slowly the young man walks to the garage hoping that they will close soon.*

Exercise 5 · Superstitions

1. Viele Menschen sind abergläubisch.

2. Sie glauben nicht wirklich an übersinnliche Dinge *(superstitions)*, aber sie wollen alle die Zukunft beeinflussen *(influence)*.

3. So sagen sie, dass etwas Schreckliches passieren wird, wenn man dies oder das tut.

4. Viele Leute fürchten sich vor Freitag, dem dreizehnten.

5. Sie glauben, dass sie Unglück haben werden, wenn eine schwarze Katze ihren Weg kreuzt.

6. Aber wenn wir nicht an diese Dinge glauben, wird uns nichts Schlechtes passieren.

Unit 11   Prejudices

Exercise 1 · Where do they work?

Write sentences about the following people. The words in the boxes will help you.

1. ~~teacher~~
2. nurse
3. policeman
4. secretary
5. electrician
6. farmer
7. plumber
8. lawyer
9. musician

play music   fix bathroom equipment
do legal work   ~~help students~~
look after patients   do organisation
install electrical equipment
keep traffic going   look after animals

office   hospital
recording studio
farm   house
court room   building
streets   ~~classroom~~

1. *A teacher helps students in a classroom.*
2. *A nurse* _____ .
3. _____ .
4. _____ .
5. _____ .
   _____ .
6. _____ .
7. _____ .
8. _____ .
9. _____ .

Exercise 2 · A job interview

2 a) A German firm is looking for a young person with excellent English to work for them in Britain.
In the following part of the job interview between the interviewer (I) and the candidate (C) the words in the box are missing. Fill them in.

just   ever   never   yet

I   By the way, where did you see our advertisement for this job?
C   It was in the local newspaper.
I   Oh, yes. Now, have you (1) _____ worked in Britain before?

50 ■ *fifty*

C No, I haven't. In fact, I haven't had a job anywhere abroad (2) _____ but I've (3) _____ come back from England. I was on holiday there. It was very interesting and while I was there I thought it would be nice to get a job in Britain. And then I saw your advert in the paper.

I Have you (4) _____ been to Scotland? You know the job is in Glasgow?

C No, I have (5) _____ visited Scotland, but I am sure I would be happy there.

I Do you think you will be able to understand the people there?

C Well, I think so. You see, I've (6) _____ finished a course in Business English at college and our teacher was a Scotsman. He gave us a lot of tips.

2 b) Fill in the correct form of the verb.

	Infinitive	Past Simple	Present Perfect
1.	to think		thought
2.	to see		seen
3.	to come	came	
4.		wrote	written
5.	to do	did	
6.	to spend		spent
7.	to be	was	
8.	to speak	spoke	
9.		had	had
10.	to go	went	

Exercise 3 · Have you ever …?

Complete the following sentences or questions by using the Present Perfect.

1. I write letters in English in my job. I _____ just _____ a letter in English.
2. I often speak English on the phone. _____ you ever _____ English on the phone?
3. A German friend of mine never goes abroad. He _____ never _____ to Britain.
4. My parents never visit foreign countries. They _____ never _____ any foreign countries in their lives.
5. My friends often spend their holidays in England. They _____ just _____ their holidays in the South West of England.
6. I am often in the U.S. on business. _____ you ever _____ to the U.S. on business?
7. My friend sometimes reads the newspaper 'The European'. She _____ just _____ an article on racial prejudice.
8. She also watches films in English. _____ you ever _____ a film in English?

11

Exercise 4 · Clues for hidden words

The hidden words in 19 Down mean "the same chances for everybody".

1. The firm asked me to come to a job ...
2. Certificates, reports etc.
3. Taking ... can be very dangerous.
4. I am innocent. It is not my ...
5. If you are unwilling to work, people call you ...
6. Legal ending of a marriage
7. For the new job I wrote a letter of ...
8. Person who gives work to people
9. Things that belong to you are your ...
10. Foreigners are often victims of ...
11. Saying what you do not like about something or someone
12. Someone who cannot find a job is ...
13. Not being the same
14. Stealing is a ...
15. Women often believe they are ... of prejudice.
16. Some employers ... against women.
17. Asking strangers for money or food
18. Not showing responsibility

Exercise 5 · Prejudices

Translate the following sentences into English.

1. Ein Vorurteil ist etwas, woran wir glauben, das wir aber nicht beweisen können.

2. Die folgenden Sätze sind typische Beispiele für Vorurteile.

3. „Frauen sind schlechtere Autofahrer als Männer."

4. „Männer sind kreativer als Frauen."

5. „Junge Leute, die auf der Straße betteln, sind faul und wollen nicht arbeiten."

6. „Die ältere Generation hat wenig Verständnis (*understanding*) für die jüngere Generation."

7. Wir haben gerade einen interessanten Artikel über solche Vorurteile gelesen.

8. Ich habe noch nie über solche Probleme in unserer Gesellschaft gesprochen.

9. Hast du schon einmal darüber nachgedacht?

10. Was können wir tun um unsere Einstellung (*attitudes*) zu ändern?

Unit 12   What's on?

Exercise 1 · What's on the box?

1 a) Put the letters of the words in the bubbles below into the right order to find the names of some of the programmes you can watch on TV.

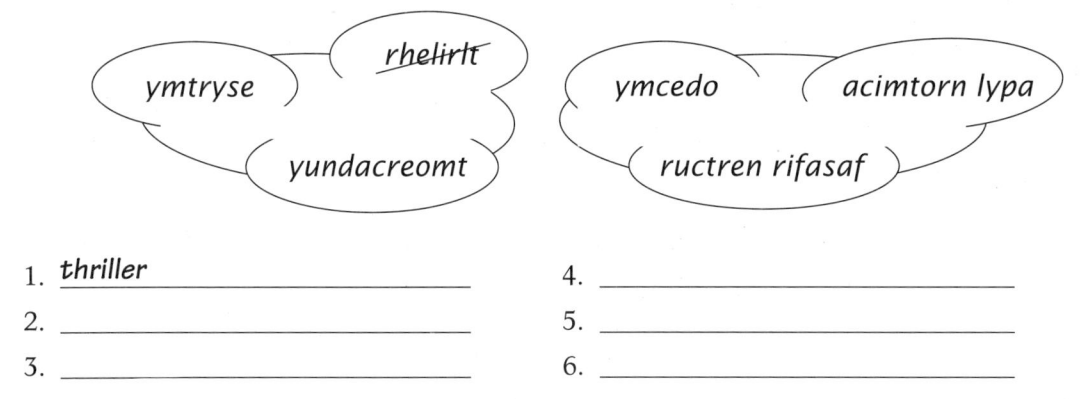

bubbles: ymtryse, rhelirlt, yundacreomt, ymcedo, acimtorn lypa, ructren rifasaf

1. _thriller_
2. _____
3. _____
4. _____
5. _____
6. _____

1 b) Now use one of the words above with a suitable word from the box below to make complete sentences.

> funny   sentimental   _frightening_
> boring   interesting   exciting

1. 'Ghost House' sounds like a __thriller__ to me, I don't like them, they're __frightening__.
2. 'Stranger in the Park' could be a _____, I like them, they're _____.
3. 'Love Story' sounds like a _____ to me, I don't like them, they're _____.
4. 'Monty Python' may be a _____, I like them, they're _____.
5. 'The World this Weekend' sounds like a _____ programme to me, I don't like them, they're _____.
6. 'The Nation's Homeless' could be a _____, I like them, they're _____.

Watching the Rocky Horror Picture Show …

Exercise 2 · What the critics choose

Read these reviews of programmes which people can see on TV tonight.
Fill in the gaps with *who*, *which* or *that*.

1. Trouble at the Top – BBC 2 at 9.50 pm
   A Claire Smith film ___which/that___ tells the story of a man _____ owns an exclusive fitness studio _____ is making a lot of money.

2. Secret Lives: Madonna – Channel 4 at 9 pm
   A woman _____ is always in the news and a programme _____ tries to show the person _____ is behind the public face.

3. Classic Trains – Channel 4 at 10.30 pm
   This is a series _____ I really like watching and tonight's programme, _____ is about trams, appeals to me a lot.

4. Great Orchestras of the World – BBC 1 at 6.30 pm
   We tour with a group of musicians _____ I think are the best in the world and hear music by composers _____ have given listening pleasure to millions over the years.

5. Young Talent – ITV at 8 pm
   A report about promising young footballers _____ play for clubs _____ don't always treat them well.

6. Tales of Mystery – ITV at 11 pm
   The final episode, _____ I am looking forward to a lot, from the woman _____ is Britain's greatest mystery writer. Can the man _____ owns the boat on the Thames really be the killer? This is one of the better programmes _____ ITV is showing tonight.

Exercise 3 · How long ago?

3 a) Add *for* or *since* to these expressions of time.

1. _____ 1957
2. _____ last Christmas
3. _____ three years
4. _____ she got married
5. _____ his birthday
6. _____ months
7. _____ a year
8. _____ Sunday
9. _____ two weeks ago
10. _____ over a year

3 b) Rewrite these sentences using the Present Perfect of the verb in brackets and either *for* or *since*.

1. Nick first met Jane last year. (know)
   Nick has known Jane since last year.

2. Sue went to America three years ago. (be)
   Sue hasn't been to America for three years.

3. John Davies last spoke to Lizzie two days ago. (speak)
   _____.

4. Sue first got interested in cooking in 1991. (be interested)
   _____.

5. Pam Wright wrote to her cousin last year. (write)
   _____.

6. Laura Perry last had a meal out months ago. (have)
   _____.

7. Steve first bought a car in 1996. (have)
   _____.

8. My sister gave up smoking two months ago. (smoke)
   _____.

9. Lizzie started her diet last month. (be on a diet)
   _____.

10. Pete lost his job in April. (work)
    _____.

Exercise 4 · Around the box

4 a) Below are some definitions of the kinds of programme you can see on TV. Find the words and fill them in on the screen.

1. _____
2. _____
3. _____
4. _____
5. _____

1. a group of programmes that are all of the same kind
2. a programme where the events shown happened in the past
3. a programme which they have shown before
4. one programme in a number of programmes which tell a story
5. a continuous story which they show regularly in parts

4 b) One word in each of the following sentences makes no sense.
Cross it out and replace it with the correct word.

1. That horror film last night was terrible, it was full of dead ~~houses~~. _corpses_
2. In the programme 'Classical Favourites' tonight at 9 pm you can hear music by many well-known centenaries. _____
3. Tonight there is a life concert from the Albert Hall. _____
4. This programme is boring, let's switch to another episode and see what they're showing. _____
5. I won't be in tonight so I've asked Danny to repeat the programme I want to watch. _____
6. I love wild animals so I mustn't miss the comedy programme tonight. _____
7. The comedy series 'Friends' is so funny you can hear the screams from the neighbours next door. _____

Exercise 5 · A favourite soap

Translate the following sentences into English.

1. Reg, der in dieser Fortsetzungsgeschichte von John Merchant gespielt wird, hat Carol vor zwei Wochen verlassen. _____
2. Ihr Leben ist seitdem zu einem Alptraum geworden. _____
3. Ihre Mutter, die behindert ist, versucht seit zwei Wochen der Sache auf den Grund zu gehen. _____
4. Aber Reg möchte seine Frau im Unklaren lassen. _____
5. In der Kneipe 'Dirty Dog', die an der Ecke ihrer Straße ist, trifft Carol eines Abends einen rätselhaften Fremden, der ihr erzählt, dass Reg Schwierigkeiten mit der Polizei hatte. _____
6. Inzwischen klagen die Einwohner der Factory Street darüber, dass das Haus Nr. 19 ein Geisterhaus geworden ist. _____
7. Die nächste spannende Folge, die alles Geheimnisvolle *(mysteries)* klären wird, wird heute Abend um 19.30 Uhr gezeigt. _____

Unit 13 In black and white

Exercise 1 · Spelling

1 a) Complete the sentences below with a word that has one of the double consonants or double vowels listed in the box.

| bb | cc | ee | ll | mm | nn | ~~oo~~ | pp | ss | zz |

1. If you have to match words, you must __choose__ the words which belong together.
2. _____ is one of the girl's names in INTERWAY.
3. Most people do not normally work at the _____.
4. The _____ left the bank with one million pounds.
5. Fashion designers usually show their new clothes _____ in spring and autumn.
6. The weather tomorrow will be fine because of high _____.
7. There was a traffic jam yesterday because of a terrible road _____.
8. Rod's article is so _____ that it makes a lot of people laugh.
9. Elaine isn't as fat as other people. She's _____ than most.
10. If you do not know that something is true but you believe that it could be true then you _____ it is true.

1 b) In each of the following words two vowels (a, e, i, o, u) are missing. Fill them in.

1. w_ea_ther
2. br___kthr___gh
3. Parl___ment
4. surg___n
5. p___rs
6. h___dline
7. to rec___ve
8. to r___ch
9. grapefr___t
10. fash___n
11. tr___tment
12. ___rthquake
13. stor___s
14. sc___ntist
15. sold___r
16. id___s
17. s___tcase
18. fl___d
19. open-___r
20. g___l
21. to l___gh

1 c) Which sentence is hidden here?

→ YOUC ARNT CH-T ITHA TYPI NGTU TALK HICH STOY OU.
ANLE OTOU YPEW TORW

Exercise 2 · Missing links

Complete the sentences below with a suitable word from the box.

| to | at | with | about | to | up | for | with | in | away |

Nick isn't interested (1) _____ newspapers. Rod is talking (2) _____ Nick. "Look (3) _____ this headline," he says. "This article is (4) _____ a man who robbed Midlands Bank. He got (5) _____ (6) _____ one hundred thousand pounds. The man is responsible (7) _____ the death of an old woman. The ambulance took her (8) _____ hospital but it was too late." Nick isn't listening. He is fed (9) _____ (10) _____ all these articles.

Exercise 3 · Have you ever …? When …?

A reporter from the newspaper 'Berlingske Tidende' asks your Danish friend Helle questions about her experiences with English-speaking countries. Write down the questions and answer them. Use the words given.

1. meet anyone from America here in Denmark – a month ago
   Have you ever met anyone from America here in Denmark? – Yes, I have.
   When did you meet them? – I met them a month ago.

2. visit the USA – last year
   _____
   _____

3. read a newspaper in English – during the holidays
   _____
   _____
   _____

4. hear an Australian pop group – yesterday
   _____
   _____
   _____

5. see a film in English – at school last week
   _____
   _____

6. take part in a school exchange abroad – when I was 15
   _____
   _____
   _____

7. have guests from an English-speaking country – two months ago

   _____
   _____
   _____

8. stay in an English-speaking country for some weeks – in my last holidays

   _____
   _____
   _____

Exercise 4 · Working with words

4 a) Complete the following list of verbs and nouns.

verbs	nouns
	development
live	
	payment
record	
	dictation
invent	
	organisation
solve	
	information
publish	
	decision

4 b) Now fill in one of the above words in the correct sentence. If you use a verb, put it into the correct tense.

Life starts at 90!

When Andrew Masters lost his sight, he (1) _____ to learn to type and to write the story of his (2) _____. First he wanted to (3) _____ his ideas to his wife, but he knew he could only (4) _____ his thoughts on paper. Now he has found a (5) _____ to his problem. His son has (6) _____ a special kind of software. Some people say that soon a top UK company will (7) _____ Andrew's book and that they have already (8) _____ a large advance.

60 ■ sixty

Exercise 5 · What has happened?

Answer the following questions. Use the Present Perfect.

1. Why don't you telephone your friend? (forget – number)
   Because I've forgotten his number.

2. Why don't you open the door? (lose – key)
   _____.

3. Why can't you go to work? (break – leg)
   _____.

4. Why don't you pay the bill? (lose – credit card)
   _____.

5. Why are you still here? (miss – bus)
   _____.

6. Why can't you read that? (forget – glasses)
   _____.

7. Why do you have so much money? (win – lottery)
   _____.

Exercise 6
Living with a handicap

Translate the following newspaper article into English.

(1) ***Du bist niemals zu alt!***

(2) Andrew lebt in einem Reihenhaus in London. (3) Er ist seit einem Jahr blind. (4) Sein Sohn Richard hat eine spezielle Software für ihn entwickelt. (5) Andrew kann nun seine Memoiren in den Computer eintippen. (6) Er hat ein interessantes Leben geführt. (7) Andrew hat sein Buch fast beendet. (8) Ein großer Verleger hat ihm bereits eine Menge Geld bezahlt. (9) Dies wird Andrew helfen, seine Rechnungen zu bezahlen.

1. _____.
2. _____.
3. _____.
4. _____.
5. _____.
6. _____.
7. _____.
8. _____.
8. _____.
9. _____.

Unit 14 Rules and regulations

Exercise 1 · Playing the game

1 a) Match the items in the box with the definitions below.

> club   net   glove   helmet
> boots   basket   ball   bat

1. A sportsman wears it on his head.
   _____

2. A sportsman wears them on his feet.
   _____

3. It's often made of string, it's long and straight and there are holes in it. _____

4. A sportsman wears it on one hand. _____

5. It's round and it rolls easily. _____

6. It's often made of string, it's round and there are holes in it. _____

7. It's long and thin with a heavy piece at the bottom. _____

8. It's made of wood and is fatter at the bottom than at the top. _____

1 b) Put the sentences right. Use one of the words in the box above.

1. Golf players use a bat.
   Golf players don't use a bat, they use a club.

2. Tennis players need a helmet.
   _____.

3. Baseball players need a net.
   _____.

4. Football players wear a glove.
   _____.

5. Golf players need boots.
   _____.

62 ■ *sixty-two*

Exercise 2 · Sportspeople and their responsibilities

Fill in the gaps with *must* or *mustn't*.

1. The captain _____must_____ be able to lead the team on the field.
2. The referee _____ help one team and not the other.
3. The manager _____ be in control of the team.
4. The spectator _____ pay to watch big games.
5. The trainer _____ make sure that the players practise.
6. The keeper _____ let the ball into the net.
7. The attacker _____ always try to get the ball into the net.
8. The players _____ forget to turn up for a match.

Exercise 3 · Baseball

3 a) In the following text the lines are in the wrong order.
Put them in the same order as the text in your Student's Book.

☐	he is out.
☐	To play baseball you need
☐	infield and an outfield, four diamond-shaped
☐	The pitcher, who is one of the fielding team,
2	first introduced in 1846.
☐	this ball and run at least to first base.
☐	Baseball is now a popular game
☐	as many runs as possible in nine innings.
☐	played in England.
☐	There are nine players in
☐	the other fields.
☐	The batter must try to hit
☐	The area where you play has an
☐	throws the ball to the first batter.
☐	A strike ball must be below the batter's
☐	If, for example a batter misses three strike balls,
1	Modern baseball rules were
☐	bases and a small mound in the middle.
☐	each team.
☐	The aim is for the batters to score
☐	a wooden bat, a ball made of cork, and leather
☐	One team bats and
☐	armpits and above his knees.
☐	Before 1700 a game with the same name was
☐	in the US, Japan and some European and Latin American countries.
☐	gloves for the fielders.

3 b) Fill in the gaps with a suitable word.

In last night's (1) __baseball__ game against the Miami Giants, the New York Monsters (2) _____ 200 (3) _____ after nine (4) _____ and so won the (5) _____. Pete York, New York's (6) _____, threw a record number of (7) _____ balls and put the Miami (8) _____ out in a very short time. When batting themselves, the New York Monsters kept the (9) _____ in the outfield pretty busy and scored a good number of (10) _____ runs.

Exercise 4 · At the video club

Translate the following sentences into English.

1. Guten Abend. Kann ich für heute Abend ein Video ausleihen?
   _____
   _____?

2. Kein Problem. Sind Sie schon Mitglied des Clubs?
   _____
   _____?

3. Nein, noch nicht. Kann ich jetzt sofort Mitglied werden?
   _____?

4. Selbstverständlich. Sie müssen aber einen Mitgliedsbeitrag von £15 bezahlen.
   _____
   _____.

5. Muss ich auch bezahlen um das Video auszuleihen?
   _____?

6. Ja. Sie müssen pro Video £2 bezahlen, aber Sie müssen es nicht am nächsten Tag wiederbringen. Sie können es zwei Tage behalten.
   _____
   _____
   _____.

7. Sehr schön. Kann ich alles zusammen mit Scheck bezahlen?
   _____?

8. Ja, aber ich brauche erst Ihren Führerschein – als eine Art Ausweis (*identification*), wissen Sie!
   _____
   _____.

Exercise 5 · House rules

Jane and Sue are still having problems with the housework, so Sue has hung up a set of rules and marked them to show what Jane

must **!** mustn't **✗** can **✓** or needn't **—** do.

Read the rules and then make sentences using *must*, *mustn't*, *needn't* or *can*.

Dos and Don'ts for Jane

1. Do the washing up after each meal. **!**
2. Don't forget to empty the dishwasher. **✗**
3. Do Sue's washing up. **—**
4. Have as many cups of coffee as you like. **✓**
5. Do your own ironing. **!**
6. Don't leave your washing in the bath. **✗**
7. Clean Sue's room. **—**
8. Don't leave the bathroom in a mess. **✗**
9. Do Sue's ironing. **—**
10. Watch TV as often as you like. **✓**
11. Prepare Sue's supper. **—**
12. Clean the bathroom on Saturdays. **!**
13. Don't forget to take the rubbish out. **✗**
14. Read the newspaper for as long as you like. **✓**

1. *Jane must do the washing up after each meal.*
2. *Jane mustn't forget to empty the dishwasher.*
3. *Jane needn't do Sue's washing up.*
4. *Jane can have as many cups of coffee as she likes.*
5. _____
6. _____
7. _____
8. _____
9. _____
10. _____
11. _____
12. _____
13. _____
14. _____

Unit 15 — Success and failure

Exercise 1 · Inventions

1 a) Find ten inventions. Use the syllables below on the right.

1. c_____ _____ c
2. c_____ r
3. d_____ r
4. l_____ b
5. p_____ _____ e
6. r_____ o
7. refrigerator
8. t_____ e
9. t_____ n
10. v_____ _____ r

a – bulb – chine – com –
com – cord – di – dish –
disc – e – e – e – er – er – er –
er – frig – ing – light – ma –
o – o – pact – phone – print –
put – ra – re – re – sion – tel –
tel – tor – vi – vid – wash

1 b) Use words from **1 a)** to say what was invented when or by whom. Use the verbs in brackets.

1. The __radio__ __was invented__ by an Italian. (invent)
2. The _____ _____ first _____ by Sony. (produce)
3. The _____ _____ by an Australian. (develop)
4. The first _____ _____ in the 18th century. (invent)
5. The _____ _____ first _____ by Gutenberg. (build)
6. The _____ _____ by Edison in 1876. (develop)

Exercise 2 · Useful verbs

2 a) Look at the verbs in the box below. Decide whether they are regular or irregular verbs. Then write their third form (Past Participle) in the list on the right.

make   predict   think   keep
build   use   fly   invent
add   begin   power
know   manufacture   fill

Regular verbs	Irregular verbs
predicted	made

2 b) Use a suitable verb from your list on page 66 to complete the following text.

Road transport

Many inventions were (1) ____predicted____ hundreds of years before they were actually (2) _____. The first bicycle was (3) _____ in Scotland in 1839 but it was not very comfortable and safe. So it was only (4) _____ by few people. About fifty years later brakes were (5) _____ and the tyres were (6) _____ with air. At that time the first tricycles were (7) _____ by petrol engines. In 1885 the first Benz car was (8) _____. This year is still (9) _____ as the start of a revolution in private transport. Millions of cars have been (10) _____ since then. Some people say that in the future cars will not have wheels any more and will be (11) _____ by their drivers some centimetres above the road.

Exercise 3
The development of transport

Put the following sentences into the passive voice. Leave out the *by-agent* if possible.

1. In the 15th century Leonardo da Vinci made the first sketch of a helicopter.
2. Men made the first flight in a hot-air balloon in 1783.
3. In the 19th century people kept the dream of flying alive.
4. In 1907 the Wright Brothers made the first successful aeroplane flights.
5. Yuri Gagarin manned the first flight into space in 1961.
6. Some people revived ballooning as a sport some years ago.
7. Companies have installed moving walkways so that people needn't walk.
8. You can see them in many airports.
9. Perhaps someone will invent the moving pavement soon.

1. _The first sketch of a helicopter was made by Leonardo da Vinci in the 15th century._
2. _The first flight_ _____.
3. _____.
4. _____.
5. _____.
6. _____.
7. _____.
8. _____.
9. _____.

Exercise 4 · The new bridge

Perhaps the following article will be published in an electronic newspaper in 20 years' time. Translate the text into English.

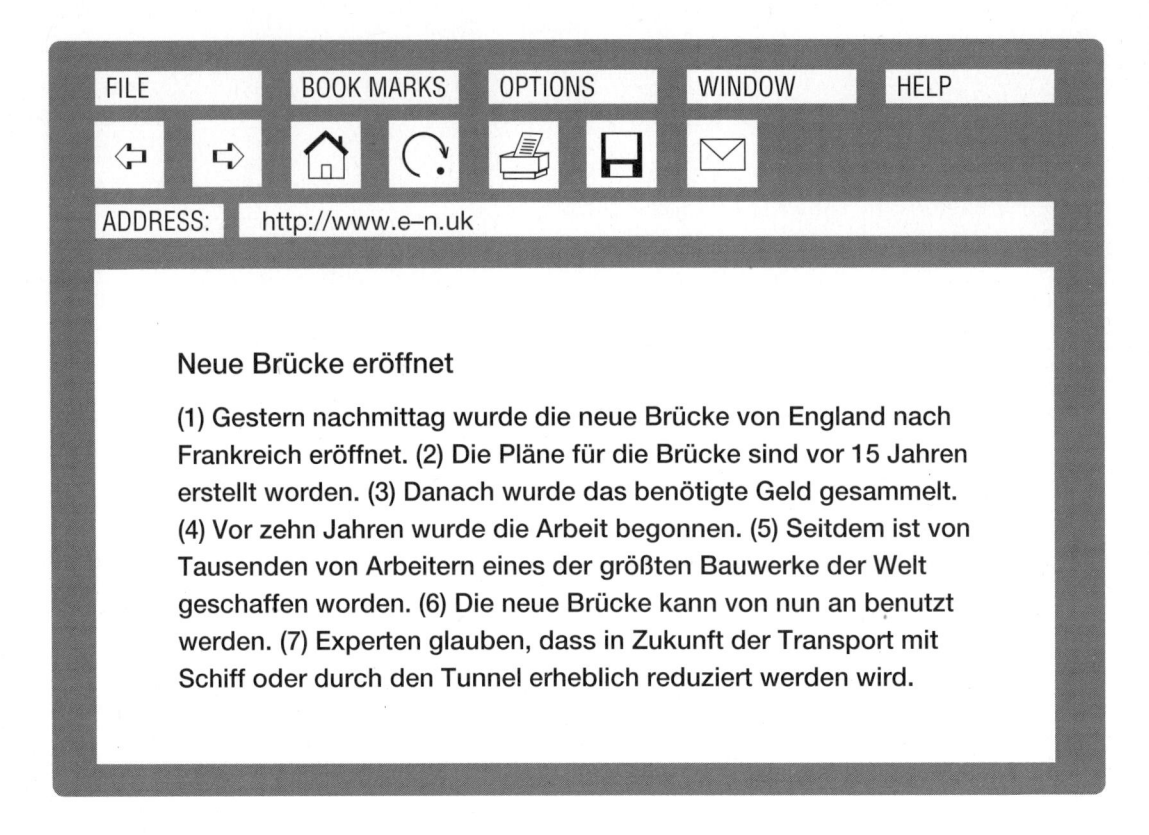

ADDRESS: http://www.e–n.uk

Neue Brücke eröffnet

(1) Gestern nachmittag wurde die neue Brücke von England nach Frankreich eröffnet. (2) Die Pläne für die Brücke sind vor 15 Jahren erstellt worden. (3) Danach wurde das benötigte Geld gesammelt. (4) Vor zehn Jahren wurde die Arbeit begonnen. (5) Seitdem ist von Tausenden von Arbeitern eines der größten Bauwerke der Welt geschaffen worden. (6) Die neue Brücke kann von nun an benutzt werden. (7) Experten glauben, dass in Zukunft der Transport mit Schiff oder durch den Tunnel erheblich reduziert werden wird.

New bridge opened

1. ___
2. ___
3. ___
4. ___
5. ___
6. ___
7. ___

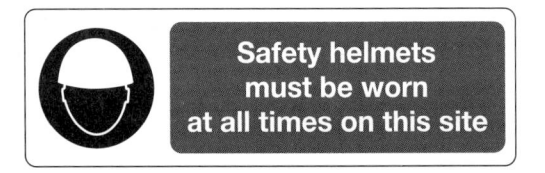

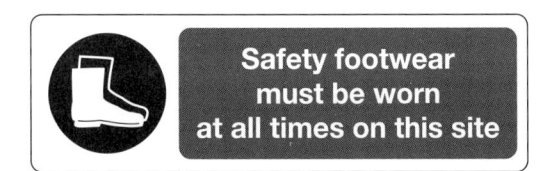

Safety helmets must be worn at all times on this site

Safety footwear must be worn at all times on this site

Unit 16 — Does age matter?

Exercise 1 · At the age of 16

Look at the following pictures and then write sentences about what you are allowed and what you are not allowed to do when you reach the age of sixteen in Britain.

1. You are not allowed to give blood.
2. _____.
3. _____.
4. _____.
5. _____.
6. _____.
7. _____.

sixty-nine ■ 69

16

Exercise 2 · Adjectives and adverbs

2 a) Complete the table by filling in the adjectives or the adverbs.

	Adjective	Adverb
1.	quiet	quietly
2.	slow	
3.		badly
4.	hard	
5.	good	
6.		quickly
7.		politely
8.	careful	
9.	terrible	
10.	fast	

2 b) Nathalie is a French trainee working in Liverpool.
Here are some remarks that people in Nathalie's firm have made about her.
Change the sentences by using adverbs instead of adjectives.

1. Nathalie has always been careful about checking everything.
   Nathalie has always checked everything carefully.

2. She is always polite to guests.
   She always deals with guests _____.

3. Her English is good.
   She speaks _____.

4. She is a quick learner.
   _____.

5. She is a fast driver.
   _____.

6. She is a slow typist.
   _____.

7. She has always been a hard worker.
   _____.

8. Unfortunately, she is a bad communicator on the phone.
   _____.

Exercise 3 · Sam's terrible day

Write complete sentences from the following prompts.
Use both the Past Simple and the Past Perfect tenses.

1. the alarm clock – ring at 9 o'clock – because – he not set it correctly
   The alarm clock rang at 9 o'clock because he had not set it correctly.

2. when – he arrive at the station – his train already leave

3. by the time – he come to the office – his boss ask for him several times

4. Later, when – he want to pay for his lunch – he realise – he leave his wallet at home

5. Luckily, – he find a £5 note in his pocket – which he put in there in the morning

6. on his way back to the office in the rain – he remember – he forget his umbrella

7. by the time – he arrive back at the office – several important people already want to speak to him

8. by 4 o'clock in the afternoon – he realise – he develop an allergy

9. he decide to go to the chemist's – after he finish work

10. but when – he want to pay for the tablets – he remember again – he leave his wallet at home

16

Exercise 4 · Words in a maze

4 a) There are 13 words from the text in the Student's Book (page 106) hidden in the box below. Look at the maze (*Irrgarten*) in the box on the right. To find each word, start at the little star in the maze and follow the letters to the end.

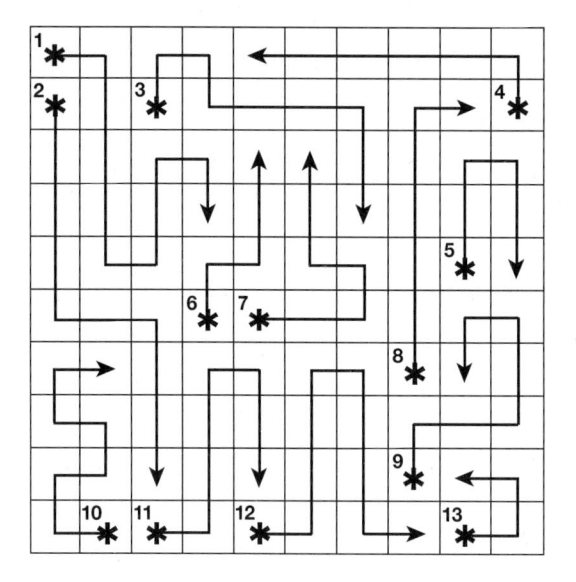

1 D	E	N	F	H	G	U	O	R	H
2 A	V	3 I	L	U	E	N	U	S	4 T
P	E	E	N	E	R	C	O	S	U
P	L	M	T	C	A	E	I	A	A
E	O	P	O	I	L	U	R	5 C	L
A	R	A	6 V	7 P	O	P	E	T	A
I	A	N	E	N	P	T	8 S	E	N
R	E	C	I	C	E	A	O	M	I
S	T	E	D	E	C	B	9 D	L	L
Y	10 H	11 A	U	12 A	C	L	E	13 D	U

1. _____
2. _____
3. _____
4. _____
5. _____
6. _____
7. _____
8. _____
9. _____
10. _____
11. _____
12. _____
13. _____

4 b) Fill in suitable words from **4 a)** in the sentences below.

1. The Beatles were very _____ in the sixties.
2. They had a great _____ on pop music.
3. Before their time pop music had been very _____.
4. Soon they were well-known _____ their concert tours.
5. Even _____ musicians played their music.
6. Wherever they made an _____ there was _____: *Beatlemania* had begun.
7. Wherever they played, the _____ was crazy about them.
8. The Beatles made pop music _____ to everyone.

Exercise 5 · Growing up

Translate the following sentences into English.

1. Bis (*By the time*) ich 20 war, hatte ich mehrere Schulen besucht.

2. Ich war immer ein schlechter Schüler gewesen.

3. Ich konnte nicht so schnell lernen wie meine Freunde.

4. Nachdem ich meinen Zivildienst (*social service*) im Altenheim (*old people's home*) gemacht hatte, interessierte ich mich mehr für ältere Menschen und ihre Probleme.

5. Die Arbeit im Altenheim war nicht so schwierig wie ich erwartet hatte.

6. Ich nahm meine Arbeit dort sehr ernst.

7. Niemand sollte sagen, dass junge Menschen nicht Positionen mit Verantwortung einnehmen (*have*) können.

8. Natürlich haben auch jüngere Leute Vorurteile gegenüber älteren Menschen.

9. Aber wir sollten uns daran erinnern, dass wir alle älter werden und eines Tages vielleicht Hilfe brauchen.

10. Nachdem ich meinen Zivildienst beendet hatte, beschloss ich, Pfleger (*nurse*) in einem Altenheim zu werden.

Unit 17 — Going green!

Exercise 1 · Pollution – who cares?

1 a) Find words which have something to do with the environment from the syllables below on the right.

1. _atmosphere_
2. _____
3. _____
4. _____
5. _____
6. _____
7. _____
8. _____
9. _____
10. _____

re – at – cy – fumes –
pow – bat – fos – ing –
haust – teries – sil –
aero – fuels – ex – sols –
al – re – ing – mos –
duce – wash – ders –
glob – warm – phere –
charge – re – cling

1 b) Complete the following sentences with a suitable word from above.

1. Oil and coal for example are ___fossil fuels___.
2. We should use _____ without CFCs.
3. Already we are _____ paper, glass and tin.
4. Dangerous _____ are produced by cars.
5. Water is poisoned by _____.
6. We should buy batteries which we can _____.
7. _____ means that the earth's temperature is increasing.
8. We should _____ the amount of energy we use.

1 c) Make as many words as you can from the word ENVIRONMENT. More than 12 words is a very good result!

time – move _____
_____
_____
_____
_____

Exercise 2 · Green politics

2 a) Match the following statements about the environment with the person you think said them.

1. Pollution causes global warming.
2. Energy saving is increasing.
3. We need fossil fuels to heat our homes and run our cars.
4. Most modern aerosols don't contain CFCs.
5. We are polluting lakes and rivers with our washing powders.
6. We are already making aerosols which we can recycle.

aerosol manufacturer

Green Party member `1`

energy spokeswoman

2 b) Now report what each person said.

1. *The Green Party member said that pollution caused global warming.*
2. *She also said* _____
3. _____
4. _____
5. _____
6. _____

seventy-five ■ 75

Exercise 3 · The ozone hole

Here is part of a talk about the ozone hole.
Put the numbered sentences into Reported Speech.

> ... and (1) up until now, the ozone layer has protected the earth from the most dangerous effects of the sun.
> (2) But several years ago, scientists discovered holes in this layer.
> (3) Without ozone, crops and fish will be destroyed and skin cancer will become more common among humans.
> (4) Scientists have also discovered that the damage was caused by CFCs.
> (5) These have been used up to now, not only in aerosols, but also in the computer industry, in polystyrene boxes and in cooling systems.
> (6) In 1978 the USA stopped using CFCs, but Britain has only recently begun to realise the dangers.
> (7) Consumers can help to reduce those dangers if they do not buy goods which contain CFCs.

1. *... and the speaker went on to say that up until then the ozone layer had protected the earth from the most dangerous effects of the sun.*

2. *He said that* _____

3. _____

4. _____

5. _____

6. _____

7. _____

Exercise 4 · Shopping for an aerosol

In the following text, choose the correct word in each case and cross out the wrong ones.

It was a hot and | sunny / ~~wet~~ / ~~cool~~ | afternoon and my room was full of | scientists. / flies. / consumers.

When I looked in the | cupboard / CD player / roof | I disovered that the | fly / hair / deodorant | spray was empty.

So I decided to go to the | garbage dump / supermarket / doctor | to get some more.

On the way I passed some | policemen / farmers / workmen | who were removing | chewing gum / fingerprints / medicine |

from the | street / environment / ozone layer | and they were using an aerosol, too.

Of course, nowadays aerosols no longer contain the | aluminium / chemical / magnet | which | damages / disinfects / develops | the ozone layer.

So it's O.K. to use them. When I got to the supermarket

the shelves were full of different | surfaces / aircraft / aerosols | so I really didn't know which one to buy.

But finally I found one with the | paints / perfumes / insecticides | and paid the | woman / market researcher / American soldier | at the check out.

On the way home it started | exploding / raining / suffering | and when I got home

I found that the flies had all | been recycled. / got malaria. / gone.

17

Exercise 5 · Protecting the environment

Translate the following sentences into English.

1. Letzte Woche bin ich zu einem Informationsabend unserer örtlichen (*local*) Umweltgruppe gegangen.

2. Das Thema war 'Sprühdosen im Hause'.

3. Die Sprecherin (*spokeswoman*) sagte, dass viele Leute immer noch glaubten, Sprühdosen seien gefährlich für die Umwelt.

4. Sie sagte, seit 1990 gäbe es eine neue Chemikalie, die die Umwelt nicht schädige.

5. Ein Mitglied erklärte, es sei jetzt möglich Sprühdosen zu recyceln, obwohl dies schwierig sei.

6. Er fügte hinzu, dass es immer noch wichtig sei, so wenig Sprühdosen wie möglich zu kaufen.

7. In Zukunft, sagte die Sprecherin, würde die Industrie Dosen ohne Aluminium herstellen.

8. Dann wäre es möglich, diese Sprühdosen aus dem unsortierten Müll zu trennen.

Unit 18 · Play the game!

Exercise 1 · The computer and its parts

Choose a suitable computer part from the following box and fill it into the text below.

mouse   screen
button   microphone
CD ROM   joystick
keyboard   drive

1. You want to record sound.
   You need a __microphone__.

2. If you want to take part in a race game on the computer, you should have a _____.

3. New computer games are usually sold on _____.

4. You have to type a text. You need a _____ for that.

5. You can't see anything on your computer unless you have a _____.

6. If you want to start a game, you have to put the CD ROM into the _____.

7. You want to start a program, so you klick the left _____ of your _____.

Exercise 2 · Word families

2 a) Find the corresponding noun for the adjective or verb given.

Adjective		Noun	Verb
violent →	1.	_violence_	
	2.	_____	← build
popular →	3.	_____	
	4.	_____	← design
entertaining →	5.	_____	
	6.	_____	← manufacture
funny →	7.	_____	
	8.	_____	← report
successful →	9.	_____	
	10.	_____	← drive
topical →	11.	_____	
	12.	_____	← act

2 b) Fill in some of the adjectives, nouns or verbs from **2 a)** in the following text. Use the correct form.

Are computer games dangerous?

Some people think that there is too much (1) _____ in computer games today so that children are becoming more and more (2) _____.

Of course the (3) _____ of a computer game wants it to be (4) _____. And as he wants the game to be a (5) _____ he must make the game (6) _____. Some games give children the chance to (7) _____ a complete city.

So children can learn a lot. Other programs are as (8) _____ as cartoons. But on the other hand there have been (9) _____ of children who commit (10) _____ of violence such as kicking or even killing others after they had played computer games. Experts, however, are not sure if this is to do with those games.

Exercise 3 · Buying a computer game

Yesterday Lizzie and Rod went to a computer shop and asked the shop assistant about different computer games. Report their questions. Start each sentence with one of the phrases in the box.

> ask
> want to know
> want to find out

1. Lizzie: "Is League One an interesting game?"
   Lizzie wanted to know if League One was an interesting game.

2. Rod: "Can I play the game on my computer?"
   _____
   _____

3. Lizzie and Rod: "Can we buy this game on floppy disk?" _____
   _____
   _____

4. Rod: "Do you sell other football games?"
   _____
   _____

5. Lizzie: "Do you think that Toon Tycoon is entertaining?" _____
   _____
   _____

6. Rod: "Do I need a joystick for this game?"
   _____
   _____.

7. Lizzie and Rod: "Can you show us some other games, too?" _____
   _____
   _____.

8. Lizzie: "Is City Maker really phantastic?"
   _____
   _____.

9. Rod: "Don't you sell any action games?"
   _____
   _____.

10. Lizzie and Rod: "Isn't the game too expensive?"
    _____
    _____.

Exercise 4 · An interview with a shop owner

4 a) Last summer a British student wanted to write an article for a school magazine. She interviewed the owner of a London computer shop about computer games. You were in the shop at the time. Read the questions the student asked.

1. Who buys computer games?
2. What age are these people?
3. What are the advantages of computer games?
4. What time of the year do you sell most games?
5. Where are most computer games produced?
6. Why do boys prefer action games?
7. Which games are violent?
8. How much does an action game cost?

4 b) In the evening you told your friend about the interview. Report the questions.

1. *The student wanted to know who bought computer games.*
2. *She also asked the shop owner what age those customers were.*
3. _____
   _____.
4. _____
   _____.

eighty-one ■ 81

5. _____
   _____.

6. And _____
   _____.

7. She then _____
   _____.

8. Finally _____
   _____.

Exercise 5 · Computer games and violence

Do you remember the Here and Now magazine programme?
Translate the following sentences into English.

1. Die Moderatorin *(presenter)* sprach mit ihren Gästen über Gewalt bei Computerspielen.

2. Sie wollte von John Neville wissen, ob Computerspiele zu gewalttätig wären.

3. Dann fragte sie ihn, ob gewalttätige Spiele Kinder gewalttätiger machten.

4. Die Moderatorin wollte von John wissen, wie viele Computerspiele Gewalt enthielten *(contain)*.

5. Paula Williams meinte, dass auch Zeichentrickfilme *(animated cartoons)* Gewalt enthielten.

6. John erwiderte, dass Cartoons keine Gewalt gegen wirkliche *(real)* Menschen zeigten.

7. Paula sagte der Moderatorin, dass kleine Jungen gerne mit Spielzeugwaffen spielten.

Unit 19 · Dangerous developments

Exercise 1 · Food quiz

1 a) Find the 10 words which fit the definitions below.

1. This person doesn't eat meat. _____
2. This person sells meat and meat products. _____
3. This meat comes from a young cow. _____
4. This meat comes from pigs. _____
5. This meat has been cut up very small. _____
6. This animal produces eggs. _____
7. This is food we often eat for breakfast. _____
8. This is a spicy Mexican meal. _____
9. This is where you keep food which you want to keep cool. _____
10. This is what you call chickens which are kept outside. _____
11. This is an illness which cows can get. _BSE_____

1 b) Now choose suitable words from above to complete the sentences.

1. I cooked some lovely pork for supper last night but my friend Sarah couldn't eat it because she'd just become a _vegetarian_.
2. A lot of people don't eat beef at the moment because they're afraid of _____.
3. I called into the _____'s while I was out and got some sausages.
4. I've put the butter and the milk in the _____ to keep them cool.
5. Steve made a _____ dish for supper yesterday, I'm sure it tasted so good because he'd got the meat from a local farmer.

1 c) How many things to eat or drink are hidden in this egg?

_____

Underline the words.

CHICKEN NUT TURKEY YOGURT TEA VEAL LAMB BEEF FISH HAMBURGER RICE EGG GARLIC

eighty-three ■ 83

19

Exercise 2 · What would happen if ...?

Look at the ideas and their possible consequences below and then make Type II Conditional Sentences.

1. chickens not free-range / not eat the eggs
   If the chickens weren't free-range, I wouldn't eat the eggs.
2. I not worried about BSE / have the beef _____
3. you really hungry / not make a fuss about the food _____
4. supermarkets have fresh beef / not buy frozen beef _____
5. they not give drugs to some animals / eat meat _____
6. farming methods kinder / not be a vegetarian _____

Exercise 3 · Find the consequences!

Read the text on page 121 in the Student's Book again and then complete the following sentences using Type II Conditional Sentences.

1. If farmers didn't give their animals special diets, *the animals wouldn't grow fat quickly and they wouldn't produce so much milk.*
2. Animals wouldn't be so healthy if _____
3. If scientists didn't use genetic alteration to change the seeds, _____
4. If we didn't use preservatives or irradiation for food, _____
5. If these developments weren't thought to be dangerous, _____
6. If labels on food were more reliable, _____
7. If governments thought food produced from animals fed on genetically altered food was dangerous, _____
8. We would enjoy our food more if _____

Exercise 4 · Different ways and different kinds

4 a) Read the text on page 121 in the Student's Book to find out the following information.

1. 2 ways of preserving food   _irradiation; preservatives_
2. 3 different kinds of meat   _____
3. 2 kinds of food obtained from cows   _____
4. 2 reasons why farmers give their cows special diets
   _____
   _____

5. 3 good results of genetic alteration
   _____
   _____

6. 1 way of farming which does not use drugs or chemicals
   _____

7. 1 kind of food which the government says must be labelled
   _____

8. 2 kinds of job connected with food production
   _____

4 b) Now complete this short summary of the text.

(1) _Scientists_ have changed methods of food production and preservation because people want good quality, cheap food. So (2) _____ now can give their animals special diets and drugs. To improve food production scientists developed (3) _____ which means that seeds are changed to get the best results. To improve food preservation scientists developed (4) the _____ process which keeps food fresh.
But some people think these developments are dangerous and so some farmers now produce food by a method known as (5) _____. Also some people think that the (6) _____ on food should be more reliable because often descriptions of food are untrue.

19

Exercise 5 · Planning a menu

Translate the following conversation into English.

Sam   Rinderwahnsinn, Bestrahlung, Legebatterien, Lebensmittelvergiftung – es ist so schwierig zu wissen, was man kochen soll!
Lisa   Ich glaube, dass man *(they)* viel zu viel Getue um das Essen heutzutage macht.
Sam   Du hast Recht – und ich habe Roy und Phil für morgen zum Essen eingeladen und jetzt hat Phil mir gesagt, dass er Vegetarier geworden ist.
Wenn er nicht Vegetarier wäre, würde ich Huhn in Wein machen.
Lisa   Das kannst du jetzt vergessen. Aber du musst zugeben, dass manche Viehzuchtmethoden *(stock breeding methods)* grausam sind.
Sam   Stimmt, aber wenn wir uns ständig um das Essen Sorgen machen würden, würden wir wahrscheinlich verhungern!

Sam   _____

Lisa   _____

Sam   _____

Lisa   _____

Sam   _____

Exercise 6 · Printer's errors

Look at the following information leaflet issued by the vegetarian society:
Something must have gone wrong in the process of printing!
Find out which two letters are always missing, then fill in the missing letters in the text.

Th_ v_g_tarian soci_ty

Th_ v_g_tarian soci_ty has _xist_d sinc_ 1847. Th_ id_a was to p_rs_ad_ p_opl_ to _at v_g_tabl_s, fr_its and c_r_als inst_ad of fish and m_at. Animals s_pply only 10% (as m_at), 15% (as _ggs) and 30% (as milk) of th_ food val__ of th_ plants th_y _at. In oth_r words: a v_g_tarian di_t is th_ q_ick_st and b_st answ_r to th_ world food shortag_, _sp_cially if cooks and t_chnologists can mak_ it d_licio_s and attractiv_ as w_ll as g_tting good food val__ from it. It can b_ f_n to _at v_g_tarian dish_s ... why don't yo_ try?

Unit 20   Passport to the world

Exercise 1 · Learning on board

1 a) The following words all have something to do with learning.
List them under a suitable heading in the list below.

degree   school   course   class   student   university
attendance   college   teacher   progress   principal

Buildings	People	Work at college
		degree

1 b) Now complete the following text with suitable words from above.

Requirements for our course 'English on Board'

You must be over 15 years old and studying at a (1) _____,
(2) _____ or (3) _____ as a full-time (4) _____.
Your record of (5) _____ and (6) _____ in your
(7) _____ of study must be very good. You must have permission from your
(8) _____ to leave for three months.

1 c) Put the letters of the words below into the right order to find the things
that have to do with boats and life on board.

trop	_____
hisp	_____
werc	_____
nacib	_____
surice	_____
gayove	_____
ruhbroa	_____
threloop	*porthole*

Exercise 2 · An application

Fill in a suitable form of the verb.

Dear Sir or Madam

Re: Emigration to New Zealand

I (1 – read) _____have read_____ your leaflet about emigration and I (2 – write) _____ because I (3 – be) _____ interested in (4 – go) _____ to New Zealand.

I (5 – born) _____ in Newcastle in 1973; there I (6 – go) _____ to school for 11 years. At the age of 16 I (7 – start) _____ a two-year course at Newcastle College. After I (8 – finish) _____ college I (9 – begin) _____ to work as a technical assistant with Carlisle & Sons. At the age of 20 I (10 – go) _____ to university and (11 – study) _____ engineering for three years. Since I (12 – leave) _____ university I (13 – be) _____ _____ employed at ABM Engineering. At the moment I (14 – work) _____ in the R&D department.

I (15 – think) _____ of (16 – leave) _____ England because I (17 – look) _____ for a new opportunity. I (18 – like) _____ to emigrate to New Zealand because it is the best place in the world that I (19 – can) _____ imagine. I (20 – be able) _____ to leave England within three months.

I (21 – be) _____ very pleased if you (22 – decide) _____ to ask me for an interview. I (23 – hope) _____ (24 – receive) _____ your answer soon.

Yours faithfully

Mary S. Drowning

Exercise 3 · Imports and exports

3 a) Think of the names or general terms for the items in the pictures and list them under a suitable heading below.

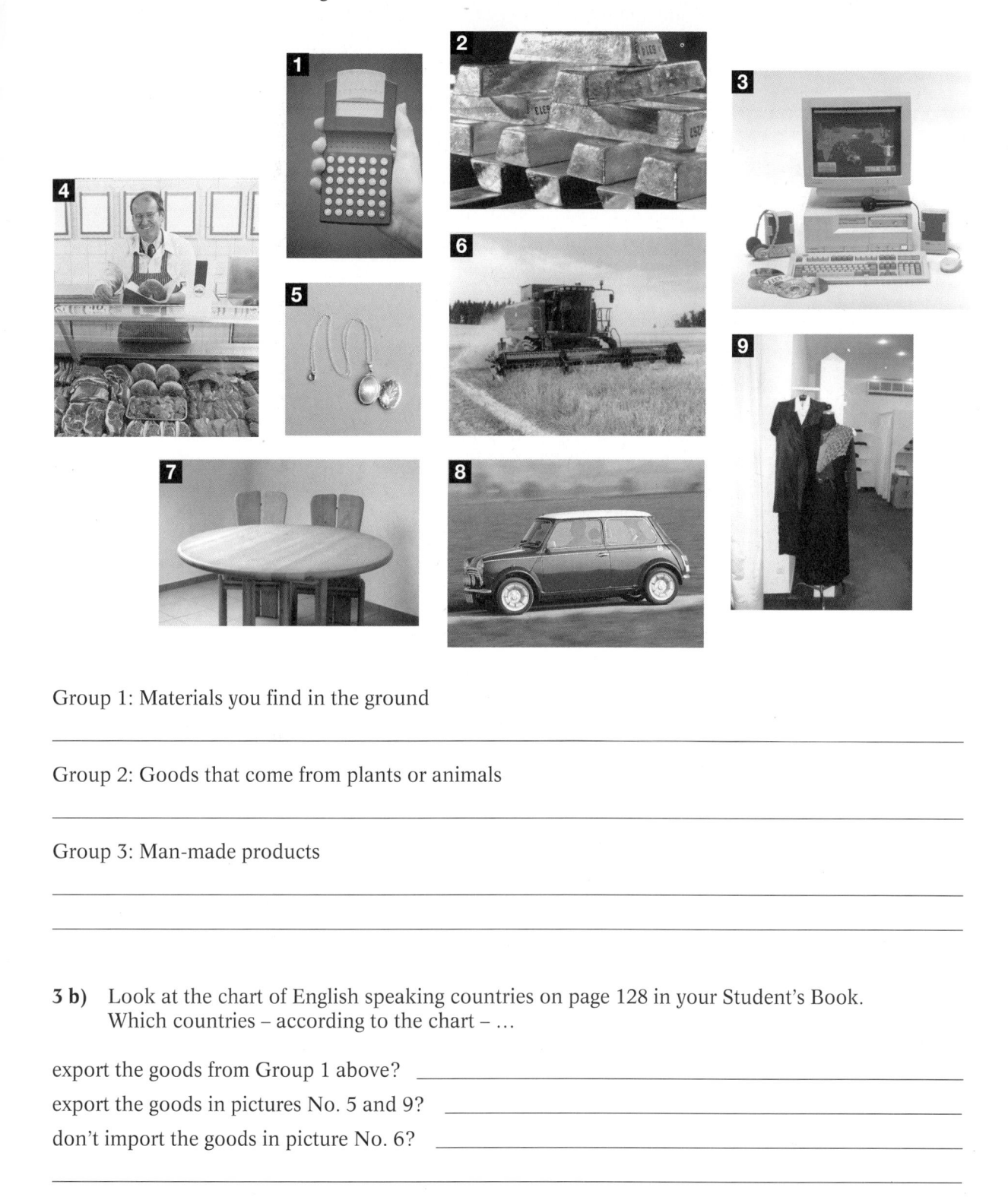

Group 1: Materials you find in the ground

_____

Group 2: Goods that come from plants or animals

_____

Group 3: Man-made products

_____

_____

3 b) Look at the chart of English speaking countries on page 128 in your Student's Book. Which countries – according to the chart – …

export the goods from Group 1 above? _____

export the goods in pictures No. 5 and 9? _____

don't import the goods in picture No. 6? _____

_____

20

Exercise 4 · Comparing English speaking countries

4 a) Compare India, South Africa, the United Kingdom and the United States with regard to size, population, population per km² and income and fill in the missing information. Refer to your Student's Book and use a pocket calculator if necessary.

Country		Size in km²		Population	Population per km²		Annual income per head in US$
US	1	9,363,123					
India	2	3,287,263	1		274		
South Africa	3	1,221,037					
UK	4	242,432					

4 b) Rank the countries in the chart according to population, population per km² and annual income per head.

4 c) Now make sentences about the No. 1 and 4 countries.

Size

1. *The US is the largest country.*
2. *The UK is* _____

Population

3. *India* _____
4. _____

Population per km²

5. _____
6. _____

Annual average income

7. _____
8. _____

90 ■ *ninety*

Exercise 5 · Learning English – the exciting way!

Translate the following newspaper article into English.

Englisch an Bord!

Gestern Nachmittag sind 120 junge Leute aus Norddeutschland mit dem Schiff in Hamburg angekommen. Nachdem sie einige Monate lang an Bord des Schiffes ‚English Traveller' gewesen waren, konnten sie die letzte Nacht zum ersten Mal wieder in ihren eigenen Betten verbringen. Kurz nach seiner Ankunft erzählte uns Mark Winter, ein Student aus Bremen, von der langen Reise: „Es begann alles vor drei Monaten. Wir verließen Hamburg und reisten zuerst nach Großbritannien, dann über den Atlantik. Jeden Tag hatten wir Sprachunterricht an Bord. Wir wurden von britischen und amerikanischen Lehrkräften unterrichtet. Bevor wir einen neuen Hafen erreichten, mussten wir ein Projekt vorbereiten. So habe ich in den letzten Monaten wirklich viel gelernt. Wenn ich die Möglichkeit bekomme, werde ich im nächsten Jahr wieder teilnehmen."

C

Commercial correspondence · Enquiry

1 Useful phrases

Opening

We refer to ...
   your advertisement in the ... of ...
   your leaflet/brochure No ...
   your sales literature.

We understand/note/learn
   that you produce/export ...
   that you have a wide range of ...

Your address has been given to us by ...

Wir beziehen uns auf ...
   Ihre Anzeige in ... vom ...
   Ihr Informationsblatt/Prospekt Nr. ...
   Ihr Informationsmaterial.

Wir ersehen/haben erfahren,
   dass Sie ... produzieren/exportieren.
   dass Sie ein großes Sortiment von ... haben.

Wir haben Ihre Adresse von ... erhalten.

Particulars

We are a leading importer/wholesaler (of) ...

We are planning to ...
   extend our range of ...
   introduce new products.

We are interested in ...

We would like to know more about ...

Please state/quote your ...
   most favourable prices and terms.
   terms of payment and delivery.
   earliest date of delivery.

Could/Would you please send us/let us have ...
   your quotation for ...?
   latest/current catalogue/price list?
   a sample of your product?

If your prices/terms ...
   are competitive ...
   come up to/meet our expectations/
      requirements ...

Would you be prepared to ...
   grant us a ... % discount?

We usually place large/regular orders.

We expect a quantity discount of ... %.

Your products will sell well in ...

Wir sind ein führender Importeur/Großhändler ...

Wir planen, ...
   unser Sortiment von ... auszuweiten.
   neue Produkte am Markt einzuführen.

Wir sind interessiert an ...

Wir möchten gern mehr erfahren über ...

Bitte nennen Sie Ihre(n) ...
   günstigsten Preise und Bedingungen.
   Lieferungs- und Zahlungsbedingungen.
   frühesten Liefertermin.

Könnten/Würden Sie uns bitte ... senden?
   Ihr Angebot für ...
   Ihre(n) neueste(n) Katalog/Preisliste
   ein Probeexemplar Ihres Produkts

Wenn Ihre Preise/Bedingungen ...
   wettbewerbsfähig sind ...
   unseren Erwartungen/Anforderungen
      entsprechen ...

Wären Sie bereit, ...
   uns ... % Rabatt zu gewähren?

In der Regel erteilen wir umfangreiche/
   regelmäßige Aufträge.

Wir erwarten einen Mengenrabatt von ... %.

Ihre Produkte werden sich in ... gut verkaufen
   lassen.

Closing

We look forward to ...-ing ...

We hope to ...
   hear from you in the near future.
   receive your answer/reply soon.

Wir freuen uns (dar)auf ...

Wir hoffen, ...
   in naher Zukunft von Ihnen zu hören.
   Ihre Antwort bald zu erhalten.

2 A gap letter

Fill in the gaps in the following enquiry.

Dear Sir or (1) _____
We (2) _____ to your (3) _____ in the 'Business Review' of 10 August and we (4) _____ that you have a (5) _____ range of computer systems. As a (6) _____ importer of computer hardware in Germany we would like to (7) _____ more about your products. Please (8) _____ your terms of payment and (9) _____. Could you please (10) _____ us your (11) _____ catalogue and price list? If your prices and (12) _____ meet our (13) _____, we will place regular (14) _____.
We (15) _____ forward to (16) _____ your answer soon.
(17) _____ faithfully

3 Writing an enquiry from English prompts

Situation:
You work for Alles fürs Büro, Zum Neuen Markt 17, 04275 Leipzig and you have heard from a business friend that Hamilton & Sons, 23 Abbey Lane, Northampton, NN3 3PQ, England, produce high-quality pens. Write an enquiry. Use today's date. Mention the following details.

ask for price and terms of payment and delivery
ask for sample of EXEL 1 pen
promise large orders if quality of product is good and conditions come up to expectations
find out about quantity discount
close letter politely

4 Writing an enquiry from German prompts

Write an enquiry in English from the prompts given. Use today's date.

Situation:
Sie arbeiten für Althoff Büromaschinen, Mainkai 126, 97070 Würzburg und interessieren sich für Produkte der Firma IAO, 122 North Central Avenue, Ramsey, New Jersey 07446, USA.

Ihre Aufgabe:
Ihre Firma ist ein führender Großhändler und möchte ihr Sortiment an Büromaschinen erweitern. Sie schreiben eine Anfrage an das amerikanische Unternehmen, dessen Adresse Sie von einem Kunden erhalten haben. Sie interessieren sich insbesondere für preisgünstige Kopiergeräte (*photo copiers*) und möchten Informationen über die Qualität der Geräte haben. Sie bitten um die Übersendung des neuesten Katalogs unter Angabe der Exportpreise sowie möglicher Rabatte, da Ihre Firma größere Aufträge erteilen möchte. Sie erbitten zudem nähere Angaben zu den Lieferungs- und Zahlungsbedingungen. Falls die Geräte Ihren Erwartungen entsprechen, würde Ihre Firma bald einen Auftrag erteilen. Sie hoffen auf eine baldige Antwort von IAO.

C

Commercial correspondence · Offer

1 Useful phrases

Opening

Thank you for …	Wir danken für …
We have pleasure in sending you …	Wir freuen uns, Ihnen … zu senden.

We are pleased to send you …
  the following offer
    on the following terms.
	Gern senden wir Ihnen …
	  folgendes Angebot
	    zu folgenden Bedingungen.

As agreed/requested …	Wie vereinbart …
Please find enclosed …	In der Anlage finden Sie …
We will send … under separate cover.	Wir schicken … mit getrennter Post.

Particulars

We are willing/prepared to grant you a(n) …
  trade/introductory/quantity/cash discount.
	Gern gewähren wir Ihnen (einen) …
	  Handels-/Einführungs-/Mengenrabatt/
	  Skonto.

This offer is valid from/until …	Dieses Angebot ist gültig von/bis …

Payment should be made …
  on receipt of the goods/order.
  in advance.
	Zahlung sollte … erfolgen.
	  bei Erhalt der Ware/des Auftrages
	  im Voraus

Delivery can be carried out …	Lieferung erfolgt …

We can arrange/organize transport …
  by air/by rail/by road/by sea.
  within 30 days after receipt of order.
	Wir können den Transport … organisieren.
	  per Luftfracht/Schiene/Straße/See
	  innerhalb von 30 Tagen nach Auftragseingang

Closing

If you have any further questions, do not hesitate to contact us.	Sollten Sie weitere Fragen haben, können Sie jederzeit mit uns Rücksprache nehmen.

We hope …
  we will have the pleasure of doing business with you.
	Wir hoffen, …
	  mit Ihnen in Geschäftsbeziehungen zu treten.

We look forward to receiving your answer/order soon.	Wir freuen uns auf Ihre(n) baldige(n) Antwort/Auftrag.

2 A gap letter

Fill in the gaps in the following offer.

Dear Ms Davidson

Offer: CD players

(1) _____ for your enquiry of 4 January … We are (2) _____ to send you the following (3) _____. As agreed on the phone please find (4) _____ our latest catalogue and price list.

We are (5) _____ to grant you a (6) _____ of 15% on the list price for all orders over 100 units. Payment should be (7) _____ on receipt of the goods. Delivery can be (8) _____ within 14 days of your order.
This offer is (9) _____ until the end of this calendar year.
If you have any (10)_____, do not (11) _____ to contact us.
We (12) _____ to receiving your order soon.
Yours sincerely

3 Matching

Match the words in the two boxes.

1. willing	a) for your enquiry
2. trade	b) enclosed
3. payment	c) on the phone
4. arrange	d) further questions
5. thank you	e) to grant
6. as agreed	f) receiving your answer
7. delivery	g) discount
8. find	h) transport
9. look forward to	i) should be made in advance
10. have any	j) can be carried out

4 Writing an offer from English prompts

Situation:
You work for Neumann GmbH, Augsburger Str. 110, 01307 Dresden. You have received an enquiry from Wards Ltd, 22 Wharf Road, Manchester M4 3BT, England, about your firm's bathroom equipment. Send them an offer. Use today's date. Mention the following details.

thank Wards Ltd for yesterday's enquiry (fax)
enclosed – latest catalogue and price list
discount – 20% (introductory discount)
payment – in advance
delivery – 14 days after receipt of order
express hope of receiving Ward's order soon

5 Translation

Translate the following sentences into English.

1. Wir danken Ihnen für Ihre Anfrage vom 10. März.
2. Wie vereinbart finden Sie unsere neueste Preisliste in der Anlage.
3. Wir sind bereit, Ihnen einen Mengenrabatt zu gewähren.
4. Zahlung sollte bei Erhalt der Ware erfolgen.
5. Wir können den Transport per Luftfracht organisieren.
6. Sollten Sie weitere Fragen haben, wenden Sie sich bitte an uns.
7. Wir hoffen, mit Ihnen in Geschäftsbeziehungen zu treten.
8. Wir freuen uns auf Ihren baldigen Auftrag.

Commercial correspondence · <u>Order</u>

1 Useful phrases

Opening

Thank you for ...
   your quotation/offer of ...
   your catalogue/brochure.
   the samples you sent us.

Wir danken Ihnen für ...
   Ihr Angebot vom ...
   Ihren Katalog/Prospekt.
   die von Ihnen übersandten Muster.

Particulars

We would be grateful if you could send us ...

Für die Übersendung von ... wären wir Ihnen dankbar.

We enclose ...
   our order for the following goods/products.

In der Anlage übersenden wir ...
   unseren Auftrag für die folgenden Waren/ Produkte.

We understand that the price quoted is ...
   Ex Works.
   FOB (Rotterdam).
   CIF (Rotterdam).
   DDP.

Wir ersehen, dass der angegebene Preis ... ist.
   ab Werk
   frei an Bord (Rotterdam)
   Kosten, Versicherung, Fracht (Rotterdam)
   verzollt geliefert

We would like to place the following/ enclosed order.

Wir erteilen Ihnen hiermit den nachstehenden/ beigefügten Auftrag.

Payment will/can be made/effected/executed ...
   with order.
   on delivery/on receipt of goods.
   within 30 days after receipt of goods.
   by transfer of the invoice amount.
   by (bank) acceptance at 90 days.
   by sight draft.
   by letter of credit.
   cash against documents.
   documents against acceptance.

Die Zahlung wird/kann ... erfolgen.
   bei Bestellung
   bei Lieferung/bei Wareneingang
   innerhalb von 30 Tagen nach Wareneingang
   per Überweisung des Rechnungsbetrags
   durch (Bank) Akzept per 90 Tage
   per Sichtwechsel
   durch Akkreditiv
   Kasse gegen Dokumente
   Dokumente gegen Akzept

Prompt delivery/Delivery by the due date is essential.

Schnelle Lieferung/Lieferung bis zum Fälligkeitstermin ist unbedingt erforderlich.

We expect an additional/introductory discount of ... %.

Wir erwarten einen zusätzlichen Rabatt/ Einführungsrabatt in Höhe von ... %.

Insurance ...
   should be obtained by you.
   will be obtained by us.

Versicherung ...
   sollte von Ihnen übernommen werden.
   wird von uns übernommen.

Closing

Please confirm/acknowledge this order ...
   in due course.
   by return.

Bitte bestätigen Sie diesen Auftrag ...
   zu gegebener Zeit.
   umgehend, postwendend.

Please let us know/inform us ...
   when the goods have been shipped.
   if there is any delay in delivery.

Wir bitten um Benachrichtigung, ...
   wann die Waren versandt wurden.
   falls eine Lieferungsverzögerung eintritt.

2. A gap letter

Fill in the gaps in the following order.

Dear Mr Millson

We (1) _____ you for your offer of 10 August and (2) _____ our order for 100 fridges XA 2000 at £199 each. Payment will be (3) _____ within 10 days after (4) _____ of goods. Prompt (5) _____ is essential. We expect a quantity (6) _____ of 10%. Insurance should be (7) _____ by you.

Please (8) _____ this order in (9) _____ course and inform us when the goods have been (10) _____.

Yours sincerely

3 Writing an order from English prompts

Write a complete order from the prompts given. Use today's date.

Situation:
You work for Büroeinrichtungscenter Fritz Steiner KG, Werner Weg 23, 59077 Hamm, a wholesaler of office equipment. You have received an offer from Laura Grenfield who works in the sales department of Office File, 96 Hayward Road, Chichester, West Sussex, PO19 3PN, England. Write an order. Use today's date. Mention the following details.

- thank Office File for offer and catalogue
- place an order for ten computer desks
- price of £79 per item is quoted CIF Rotterdam
- packing should be included
- you expect delivery within four weeks after receipt of order
- promise payment against documents
- if quality of goods meets expectations: prepared to place regular orders in the future
- ask Office File to acknowledge order by return
- close letter politely

4 Writing an order from German prompts

Write an order in English from the prompts given. Use today's date.

Situation:
Sie arbeiten im Einkauf von Firnhavel & Co. und senden folgende Bestellung an Jan Kampa, Storg 42, 26131 Landskrona, Schweden.

Ihre Aufgabe:
Sie nehmen Bezug auf das Angebot, das Sie gestern erhalten haben und danken für die Übersendung der Muster. Obwohl die Preise anderer Lieferanten niedriger sind, erteilen Sie einen Auftrag für 50 Einbauküchen (*fitted kitchen*), da die Qualität dieser Produkte besser zu sein scheint. Die Ware sollte bis spätestens Ende des nächsten Monats versandt werden. Die Versicherung wird von Ihrem Unternehmen übernommen. Die Zahlung wird gegen Übergabe der Frachtpapiere erfolgen. Sie stellen bei Zufriedenheit regelmäßige Aufträge in Aussicht. Voraussetzung wäre allerdings, dass bei diesen Bestellungen ein Mengenrabatt von 10 Prozent eingeräumt wird. Sie bitten um die Bestätigung dieses Auftrags.

Commercial correspondence · Acknowledgement of order

1 Useful phrases

Opening

Thank you for your order of ... for ...	Wir danken für Ihre(n) Auftrag/Bestellung vom ... für ...
We are pleased to acknowledge/confirm your order of ...	Wir freuen uns, Ihren Auftrag vom ... bestätigen zu können.

Particulars

We are pleased to confirm ...	Wir freuen uns, ... bestätigen zu können.
We are dealing with/processing your order ... as per/according to your specifications. as requested.	Wir führen Ihren Auftrag ... aus. gemäß Ihren Angaben wunschgemäß
We will send/dispatch the goods/your order ... by rail/post/air/ship.	Wir werden die Waren/den Auftrag ... versenden. per Bahn/Post/Luftfracht/Schiff
unfortunately	leider
due to a delay	wegen einer Verzögerung
We regret to inform you that ... the items ordered are out of stock/ no longer available.	Leider müssen wir Ihnen mitteilen, dass ... die bestellten Waren nicht erhältlich/nicht mehr vorrätig sind.
We expect new stock in the next few days.	Wir erwarten den neuen Vorrat in den nächsten Tagen.
We will inform you when the consignment is ready for delivery/dispatch.	Wir werden Sie benachrichtigen, sobald die Lieferung versandfertig ist.
We can recommend an alternative supplier/offer a substitute.	Wir können (Ihnen) einen anderen Lieferanten empfehlen/einen Ersatz anbieten.

Closing

We are certain/sure that ...	Wir sind sicher, dass ...
We hope that ... you will be pleased/satisfied with ... our products will meet with your approval.	Wir hoffen, dass ... Sie mit/über ... zufrieden sein/erfreut sein werden. unsere Produkte Ihren Erwartungen/Anforderungen entsprechen werden.
Please accept our apologies for the delay.	Wir möchten uns für die Verzögerung entschuldigen.
We look forward to further orders.	Wir freuen uns auf zukünftige Bestellungen.

2 A gap letter

Fill in the gaps in the following acknowledgement of order.

Dear Mr Hill

(1) _____ you for your (2) _____ of 10th November for ten office chairs. We are (3) _____ with your order (4) _____ to your (5) _____. We will (6) _____ the goods by ship by the end of this week. We are (7) _____ that you will be (8) _____ with our products and we (9) _____ to further orders.

Yours (10) _____

3 Writing an acknowledgement from English prompts

Situation:
You work for Spaßmacher GmbH, Neustr. 47, 47198 Duisburg. You have received an order for 600 coloured balloons (*Luftballons*) from Party Poopers, 21 Maple Road, Exeter EX1 4RS, England. Write a complete acknowledgement of order from the prompts given. Use today's date. Mention the following details.

- tell Party Poopers that you are carrying out their order as requested
- goods will be dispatched by air within ten days
- you hope that Party Poopers will be satisfied with your products
- say that you look forward to repeat orders
- end letter correctly

4 Writing an acknowledgement from German prompts

Write an acknowledgement of order in English from the prompts given. Use today's date.

Situation:
Sie arbeiten für die Firma Beckstein GmbH, Aalstr. 64, 30457 Hannover. Sie haben einen Auftrag bekommen von der Firma DIY Tools Ltd, 44 Hatfield Gardens, Birmingham B14 6EY, England für 20 Bohrmaschinen (*drills*).

Ihre Aufgabe:
Sie schreiben eine Bestätigung an die englische Firma. Leider müssen Sie DIY Tools mitteilen, dass die bestellten Waren im Moment nicht vorrätig sind. Sie erwarten den neuen Vorrat innerhalb der nächsten Woche. Sie werden den Kunden informieren, sobald die Lieferung versandfertig ist. Sie hoffen, dass Ihre Produkte den Anforderungen entsprechen werden. Sie möchten sich für die Verzögerung entschuldigen.

Commercial correspondence · <u>Reminder</u>

1 Useful phrases

Opening

Further to your order of ...	Mit Bezug auf Ihre Bestellung vom ...
Further to your/our letter of ...	Mit Bezug auf Ihren/unseren Brief vom ...

Particulars

As indicated/stated in ... your order was effected/carried out on ...	Wie in ... erwähnt, wurde Ihre Bestellung/ Ihr Auftrag am ... ausgeführt.
The goods/ items were dispatched/ sent off/left our warehouse on ...	Die Waren/Artikel wurden am ... ausgeliefert.
An invoice was sent under separate cover.	Die Rechnung wurde mit getrennter Post geschickt.
Unfortunately, we have heard nothing from you.	Leider haben wir nichts von Ihnen gehört.
We have not yet received your confirmation.	Wir haben Ihre Bestätigung noch nicht bekommen.
We have not yet received payment.	Wir haben noch keine Zahlung erhalten.
Our statement of account had obviously been overlooked.	Offensichtlich ist unser Kontoauszug übersehen worden.
Your account has not been cleared.	Ihr Konto ist nicht ausgeglichen.
We should be grateful if you could ... confirm receipt of the goods. let us have your payment/send your remittance without delay.	Wir wären Ihnen dankbar, wenn Sie ... den Empfang der Waren ... bestätigen könnten. uns Ihre Zahlung ... zukommen lassen/ die Überweisung vornehmen könnten. umgehend/baldmöglichst
We must insist that you send your remittance immediately.	Wir müssen auf einer sofortigen Begleichung bestehen.

Closing

Should there have been a simple oversight on your/our part ...	Falls es sich um ein einfaches Versehen Ihrerseits/unsererseits handelt ...
Please accept this as a friendly reminder that our invoice No ... is past due.	Dieses ist lediglich eine freundliche Erinnerung an unsere Rechnung Nr. ..., die noch nicht beglichen ist.
If you have already settled the account, please disregard this reminder.	Sollten Sie die Rechnung schon beglichen haben, so betrachten Sie diese Zahlungs- erinnerung bitte als gegenstandslos.

2 Matching

Find words in the second box which have the same meaning as the corresponding ones in the first box.

1. carry out
2. as requested
3. available
4. receipt
5. further orders
6. under separate cover
7. promptly
8. further to
9. as indicated
10. oversight

a) with reference to
b) in stock
c) separately
d) as stated
e) administrative error
f) deal with
g) arrival
h) repeat orders
i) in accordance with your wishes
j) immediately

3 Writing a reminder from English prompts

Put the following prompts in a suitable order. Then write a complete reminder.

1. be grateful if
2. yours sincerely
3. invoice sent separately on
4. as indicated order effected
5. if already settled account
6. further to our letter of
7. Dear Mr James
8. goods sent 24th October
9. payment not yet received

4 Writing a reminder from German prompts

Write a reminder in English from the prompts given.

Situation:
Sie arbeiten in der Buchhaltungsabteilung der Firma Gartenideen, Blumenstr. 13 in 54293 Trier und sind für die Überwachung der eingehenden Zahlungen zuständig. Die Firma Great Little Gardens, 14 Ballyhoo Road, Dublin DB4 7TP, Ireland, hat ihre Rechnung für die Bestellung Nr. 2764 vom 18. Mai ... für 125 Gartenschirme noch nicht bezahlt.

Ihre Aufgabe:
- schreiben Sie am 20. Juni ... an die irische Firma
- Bezug auf Auftragsbestätigung und Rechnung
- Erinnerung, dass weder Lieferungsbestätigung noch Begleichung der Rechnung bei Ihnen vorliegen
- bedauern Sie dies
- Auslieferung der Waren am 20. Mai ... per Luftfracht erfolgt (Lieferschein Nr. 42678)
- Vermutung ausdrücken, dass es sich um ein Versehen handelt
- Bitte an den Kunden, den Erhalt der Lieferung zu bestätigen
- Bitte um baldige Begleichung der Rechnung (eine Woche Frist)
- baldige Antwort von Great Little Gardens erwünscht

Commercial correspondence · Complaint

1 Useful phrases

Opening

We are sorry/regret to inform you ...
We regret to say/report that ...

Leider müssen wir Ihnen mitteilen ...
Leider müssen wir Ihnen mitteilen, dass ...

Particulars

Although we ordered the goods/made the order on ...
   the goods/the consignment have/has not arrived.
   the order is still overdue.

Obwohl wir die Waren am ... bestellten/den Auftrag am ... aufgegeben haben,
   sind die Waren/ist der Auftrag /nicht angekommen.
   ist der Auftrag jetzt überfällig.

On opening/unpacking/checking your delivery of ...
   we found/discovered that ...
   the goods have given cause for complaint/were unsatisfactory.
   your consignment is not up to the standard we require.
   the goods are/were damaged/broken.
   we had received the wrong goods.
   the consignment/order was incomplete.

Bei der Öffnung/Überprüfung Ihrer Lieferung vom ...
   stellten wir fest, dass ...
   die Ware Grund zu Beanstandung gegeben hat/nicht zufriedenstellend war.
   Ihre Lieferung nicht unserem Niveau entspricht.
   die Ware beschädigt/zerbrochen ist/war.
   wir die falsche Ware erhalten hatten.
   die Lieferung nicht vollständig war.

Please/We ask you to ...
   look into/deal with this matter immediately.
   send the consignment/replacements as soon as possible.
   deliver the goods by ... at the latest.

Wir bitten Sie, ...
   diese Angelegenheit sofort zu klären.
   die Ware/Ersatzware sobald wie möglich zu senden.
   die Ware bis spätestens ... zu liefern.

Unless the consignment arrives by ...
   we will have to/be forced to ...
   cancel the order.
   look for another supplier.

Wenn die Lieferung nicht bis ... ankommt, ...
   müssen wir/sehen wir uns gezwungen,
   den Auftrag zu stornieren.
   einen anderen Lieferanten (zu) suchen.

Closing

We are sure that ...
   you will understand our position.
   you will settle the matter as soon as possible.

Wir sind zuversichtlich, dass ...
   Sie Verständnis für unsere Lage haben.
   Sie die Angelegenheit so schnell wie möglich regeln werden.

We look forward to receiving your early reply.

Wir freuen uns, baldmöglichst von Ihnen zu hören.

2 A gap letter

Dear Mr Sanders,

Order No. 2465

We (1) _____ to inform you that although we (2) _____ these goods on 14th November, they have still not (3) _____. We need these goods urgently as our stocks are low. Therefore we (4) _____ you to (5) _____ this matter as soon as possible.

Unless the (6) _____ arrives by 5th January at the latest, we will be (7) _____ to look for another (8) _____.

We are (9) _____ that you will understand our position.

Yours (10) _____

3 Writing a complaint from English prompts

Situation:
You work for Fritz und Böhmke GmbH, Klarastr. 10, 01217 Dresden. You ordered 4,000 computer discs from Computer World, 50 Harbour Highway, Singapore. When you received the goods you found that they were damaged. Write a letter of complaint from the prompts given.
The date is 3rd June ...

- you regret that order (No. 8883) of 4th May has given cause for complaint
- on opening consignment you found that half the goods were damaged
- ask Computer World to look into the matter immediately and to send replacements
- ask them to deliver the replacements by 17th July at the latest
- tell them that unless goods arrive by this date you will be forced to cancel the order
- close by saying that you look forward to their early reply

4 Writing a complaint from German prompts

Write a letter of complaint in English from the prompts given. The date is 29th November ...

Situation:
Als Mitarbeiter/in der Firma Königsfeld GmbH, Neudorferstr. 47057 Duisburg wenden Sie sich heute an die Firma China House, 10 Ladbrook Avenue, London EC2 4HY. Die Firma hat eine mangelhafte Lieferung geschickt.

Ihre Aufgabe:
Sie nehmen Bezug auf Ihre Bestellung vom 24.10. ... Leider müssen Sie der Firma China House mitteilen, dass die Lieferung nicht zufriedenstellend war. Bei der Öffnung der Lieferung am 26.11. ... stellten Sie fest, dass die bestellte Ware – 30 Ess-Service (*dinner services*) zerbrochen war. Sie bitten die Firma China House, Ersatzware sobald wie möglich zu senden. Wenn die Lieferung nicht bis spätestens 30.12. ... ankommt, sehen Sie sich gezwungen einen anderen Lieferant zu suchen. Sie sind zuversichtlich, dass die Firma China House Verständnis für Ihre Lage haben wird.

Acknowledgements · Quellennachweis

Seite 5: Graphik-Büro Böttcher & Bayer, Stuttgart
Seite 6: 1 B. Boulton, Minehead; 2 – 4 Klett-Archiv; 5 K. Schickentanz, Göppingen; 6 J. Biller, Stuttgart; 7 H.-W. Thunig, Winterbach; 8 Deutsche Grammophon Gesellschaft mbH, Hamburg; 9 Klett-Archiv; 10 K. Schickentanz, Göppingen
Seite 10: 1 + 2 K. Schickentanz, Göppingen; 3 Laura Ashley, Eindhoven; 4 + 5 K. Schickentanz, Göppingen; 6 Klett-Archiv
Seite 14: 1 B. Boulton, Minehead; 2 Klett-Archiv; 3 Daimler-Benz Aerospace Airbus GmbH, Hamburg; 4 Bundesverband des Deutschen Textileinzelhandels e.V., Köln; 5 K. Schickentanz, Göppingen; 6 Zentralverband des Deutschen Baugewerbes e.V., Bonn; 7 Klett-Archiv; 8 Zentralverband Sanitär Heizung Klima, St. Augustin
Seite 16: K. Schickentanz, Göppingen
Seite 18: Klett-Archiv
Seite 21: *o.* Graphik-Büro Böttcher & Bayer, Stuttgart; *u.* K. Schickentanz, Göppingen
Seite 23: © King Features Syndicate, New York
Seite 24: J. Winkler, Penzberg
Seite 26: 1 + 2 Klett-Archiv; 3 Ford-Werke AG, Köln; 4 Pig Bike Handelsgesellschaft mbH, Bad Mergentheim; 5 + 6 Klett-Archiv; 7 – 9 K. Schickentanz, Göppingen; 10 Klett-Archiv; 11 J. Biller, Stuttgart; 12 Grundig Vertriebs-GmbH, Fürth
Seite 33: Graphik-Büro Böttcher & Bayer, Stuttgart
Seite 37: 1 H.-W. Thunig, Winterbach; 2 + 3 K. Schickentanz, Göppingen; 4 H.-W. Thunig, Winterbach; 5 B. Boulton, Minehead; 6 H.-W. Thunig, Winterbach; 7 B. Boulton, Minehead; 8 Hüppe, Bad Zwischenahn
Seite 47: Peter Byatt, Kingston, Surrey
Seite 50: H.-W. Thunig, Winterbach
Seite 54: Aus der humoristisch-satirischen Schweizer Zeitschrift ‚Nebelspalter'
Seite 69: Graphik-Büro Böttcher & Bayer, Stuttgart
Seite 75: *li.* B. Boulton, Minehead; *re. o.* H.-W. Thunig, Winterbach; *re. u.* W. Schickentanz, Hameln
Seite 80: Bomico GmbH, Dreieich-Sprendlingen
Seite 81: K. Schickentanz, Göppingen
Seite 86: H.-W. Thunig, Winterbach
Seite 89: 1 Deutsche Telekom AG, Bonn; 2 Deutsche Bundesbank, Frankfurt; 3 IBM Deutschland GmbH; 4 CMA Centrale Marketing-Gesellschaft der deutschen Agrarwirtschaft, Bonn; 5 K. Schickentanz, Göppingen; 6 Lehmann, Würzburg; 7 K. Schickentanz, Göppingen; 8 Rover Deutschland GmbH, Neuss; 9 K. Schickentanz, Göppingen